Old Needlework Boxes And Tools

THEIR STORY
AND HOW TO COLLECT THEM

Early nineteenth century rosewood needlework box. Fitments have glass handles inset with gold filigree work, and there is a gold and crystal vinaigrette. Seven mother-of-pearl reels still contain their original cotton thread. There is a gold thimble and finger guard, pencil, earspoon and needlecase with mother-of-pearl penknife, paperknife, ruler, yard-measure, emery and thread-waxer

Old Needlework Boxes And Tools

THEIR STORY
AND HOW TO COLLECT THEM

Mary Andere

Drake Publishers Ltd : New York

ISBN 87749-085-6

Drake Publishers, Ltd
440 Park Avenue South
New York
New York 10016

Printed in Great Britain

DEDICATION

to my Mother
who has the true Victorian's love
of little things

CONTENTS

LIST OF ILLUSTRATIONS

PLATES

9

List of Illustrations

Photographs not acknowledged above are from private collections

List of Illustrations

IN TEXT

The drawings are by the author

FOREWORD

This book began, some twelve years ago, by being a simple piece of research into the history of the thimble, made when after abortive visits to several libraries I realised just how little was written about it, and that even that little was not in any one book. Gathering a paragraph here, a couple of hints there, another paragraph, half a page, elsewhere, I found that, like any other study, it became more and more interesting and led into many totally unsuspected fields. More than that, my friends became as interested as I was, and were constantly asking how I was getting on and what new information I had gleaned. Gradually the whole scope widened to include other embroidery tools and, finally, workboxes themselves in the specific form in which they finally emerged. All this meant that, when I was asked to undertake the task of collecting the material together to form a book, I was happy to do so in the hope that the subject might bring to other collectors as much enjoyment as it has brought to me. And since people who collect things are usually those who most strongly feel the link with the past, I have included details wherever possible about the early history and various associations of the different items. All of these can be studied far more fully —it will be a rewarding task—and for more detailed information in this connection I would recommend the books given in the bibliography at the end of this book, all of which I have found not only helpful, but eminently enjoyable.

CHAPTER 1

THE NEEDLEWORK BOX

Together with the teapoy, the writing-box, and the dressing-case, the needlework box played an important part in the nineteenth-century home. It was, indeed, so commonplace an item that few people gave it a second thought, or wondered how and why it had come into being. Probably then, as now, most thought simply that workboxes, such as that illustrated in the photograph on page 18, had always been ordinary household equipment.

Normally 10 to 14in long, 8 to 10in deep, and standing some 8 to 9in high, they were a convenient size to place on a small table, or upon a chest of drawers or a low cabinet. They were light enough to be carried across the room, or out into the garden, and capacious enough to hold not only various sewing implements and materials, but also the smaller pieces of work and embroidery upon which needlewomen of that time bestowed such diligent care. Made of different polished woods, of ivory, mother-of-pearl, or a variety of other materials, and frequently inlaid or carved, whether in the plain box style or the slightly more graceful casket or coffer shape, they were in themselves a pleasing ornament. When opened, the delicately coloured linings, often quilted or ruched; the various small compartments into which the interior tray was divided, with their array of coloured silks, tiny boxes and sewing necessities; and the charming sets of needlework tools on their fitted pads, were a delight to the eye. To the collector they evoke gracious pleasant drawing-rooms and an unchanging and unchangeable serenity of life unknown today.

Yet workboxes such as these were, in fact, a comparatively recent innovation, having evolved gradually, due to a variety of reasons connected with social changes, from the early part of the eighteenth century onwards. During the eighteenth century they gradually became a feature of life, but even then only amongst the wealthier or more aristocratic circles. Humbler folk still used the forms they had known for centuries, and it was not until the early part of the nineteenth century that the needlework box really began to come into its own and was, in any sense, widespread.

Before examining such boxes in detail, it may be as well to give a brief sketch of the practical reasons which necessitated their development, and see just how sewing tools had previously been housed.

BEFORE THE NEEDLEWORK BOX

One of the earliest specimens known in this country of what is often believed to be an early sewing-box, is an Anglo-Saxon circular bronze casket, about 3in high and 2½in diameter, in the British Museum. The lid is attached to the box by a short chain, in lieu of a hinge, and the top is decorated with a simple repoussé pattern. Discovered in an Anglo-Saxon cemetery at Uncleby, in the North Riding of Yorkshire, it is, like all Anglo-Saxon so-called 'workboxes', dated to the seventh century AD. It would have been worn suspended from the belt or girdle, and some similar

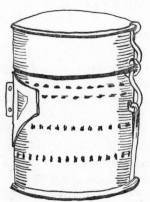

1 *Early Anglo-Saxon casket, believed to have been used as a workbox.*
(*In British Museum*)

Page 17 (above) *Stumpwork box, 1693; white satin embroidered with coloured flowers and emblems, and the Judgement of Solomon on the lid. Note lock with its fine scrollwork and finish;* (below) *typical English wooden casket, c 1830. In foreground, a fan pincushion, two leather needleboxes, needlecase and pincushion in bellows form, shell pincushion, ivory thread-waxer, reddened horn apple wax-holder, mother-of-pearl reel-holder and circular ivory pincushion*

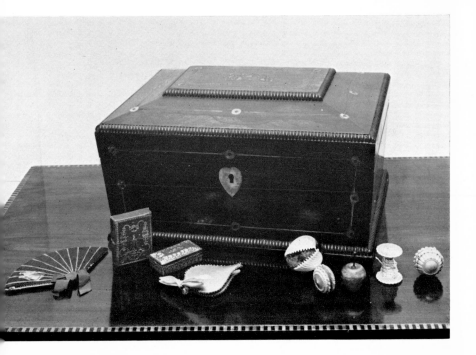

Page 18 (left) *An 18th-century worktable in walnut decorated with a floral design in marquetry. The interior, lined with deep blue silk and with blue and white compartments, is fitted with carved ivory reel-holders, emery, wax-holder and various other implements;* (below) *typical early 19th-century walnut workbox, lined with pale blue satin, with mother-of-pearl fittings. Also shown, early 19th-century leather needlebox, parasol-shaped ivory needlecase, ivory tambour hook, crochet hook with the carved figure of a mandarin, variegated shellwork yard measure and Royal Worcester thimble decorated with bullfinch flowers*

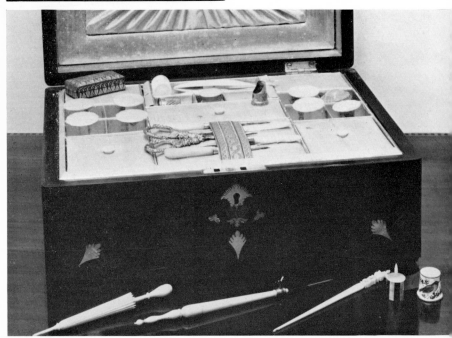

boxes still contained their needles and threads and small fragments of material when unearthed. While it is by no means certain that their original purpose was that of a sewing casket, at least those containing threads are likely to have been put to this use. Certain Continental parallels suggest rather that they may have been amulet containers for holy relics, since they are known only from Christian graves there. Certainly these caskets were the earliest way of ensuring that one's personal effects were safe and at hand, and it is probably from these that the chatelaine (page 38) eventually developed.

Since for many centuries even the simplest tools, such as needles or pins, were scarce and difficult to come by, they were treated with considerably more care and respect than they receive at our hands today, and thus for reasons of both safety and convenience it was necessary for women to carry their sewing implements about with them. In the earliest forms of garment worn in Western civilisation, pockets are non-existent, and any articles, such as combs, work tools, knives, were attached by chains or cords to the waistbands of both males and females. The Anglo-Saxon workbox clearly belonged to a woman of some rank, being made in bronze and carefully decorated. Status symbols existed even in Neolithic times, as archaeologists well know.

By medieval times ladies wore needlecases (which probably also contained pins) attached to their girdles, and these were usually made of bone or wood, though noblewomen had more elaborate ones in silver and studded with gems. A description of this type of needlecase, together with a diagram, will be found in Chapter 4. It was not until the early seventeenth century that small boxes once more came into use, and were the forerunners of the etui (page 34). These held a few needlework tools, of the most essential nature, but they were still comparatively rare and were reserved, as with all innovations, for the wealthier sections of society. Had they but realised it, this fashion was a reversion to the Anglo-Saxon lady's sewing-box, but since pockets had long since become part of normal dress, for the ordinary woman, a small sewing wallet was the usual way of keeping her sewing tools together, and was carried about in the pocket. Thomas Occleve, born about 1370, refers to such a wallet in one of his poems:

The Needlework Box

Come hyder to me, sone, and loke wheder
In this purse ther be any croise or crouche,
Sauf needel and threde and themel of lether.

Contemporary with the upright etui containing bodkins, folding scissors, needlecase and thimble; quilted and embroidered purses, wallets and pouches remained fashionable amongst the leisured classes from medieval times right up to the end of the eighteenth century. Gradually small straps were fitted into which the few and essential tools could be slotted, and the pouches were then carried about in the pocket or bag, this being very convenient since, during the eighteenth century, it was quite customary even in the highest circles for a woman to take her embroidery with her to a social gathering. Gradually, however, new varieties of needlework became fashionable, and the number and scope of sewing tools increased. Sewing bags became larger and larger, and something more permanent became necessary, until towards the end of the eighteenth century the form of workbox we are considering eventually emerged.

It was not only the size of workbags, however, which helped to bring about the change. A number of other factors also contributed, each of which, from its own especial angle, played a part in deciding the shape, form and style of workbox eventually achieved.

We are inclined to forget that for centuries people lived with very little space in which to keep their personal possessions, however few these may have been, and that pilfering and thieving were commonplace. Even as late as 1572 we find that Skipton Castle, the ancestral home of the Earls of Cumberland and one of the finest mansions in the North of England, only boasted seven or eight beds; in none of the bedchambers were there carpets, chairs or looking-glasses. From the inventory of the castle's effects we realise not how much these great and powerful families possessed, but just how much they did not have; things we take for granted in a home were unknown to them, even so far as ordinary furniture was concerned. All over Europe, anything of value, including clothing, furs, lengths of material, silver, money and jewellery, was normally all stored in the great trussing coffers or other chests which were iron-bound and fitted with a stout lock—of necessity. Examples of beautifully carved, but massively locked, coffers may be seen in London's Victoria & Albert Museum, and other less spectacular specimens abound in dozens of museums.

In the famous Paston letters, written from 1450–78, we find Dame Margaret Paston telling her husband in London that she is sending up to him his 'trussing coffer', or clothes chest, and mentioning that 'his meny rob his chamber and rifle his hutches'— hutch being the English corruption of *huche*, a French coffer or chest which stood upon legs. This brings it home to us that, at all levels of society and for many hundreds of years, the only really safe place for small personal possessions was when firmly attached to the owner's person simply because, in the majority of households, there were no small, easily accessible or portable pieces of furniture in which such items could be safely deposited. Compendiums or small coffers for various purposes were not unknown, but such items belonged to only a very small minority of the most élite society, and none of them seem, during the era in question, to have been used for sewing materials. We know that in 1562 Queen Elizabeth was presented by Sir John Alee with a richly fitted toilet case, or travelling case, as a New Year gift; it was a carved oak coffer, painted and gilded, with steel mirrors and combs and silver pomanders. Katherine of Aragon had a 'cofar having four tilles [box-like drawers] therein, the forefront of every one of them gilte'. The Victoria & Albert Museum has a fitted box of wood covered with leather, which bears the heraldic badges of Katharine and Henry VIII amidst ornate decoration in paint and gold, but such an item was for toilet necessities, or for jewellery and small valuables.

But from the middle of the seventeenth century onwards, coffers and chests developed considerably and acquired new and more elaborate forms. Bedroom furniture such as chairs, stools, tables, toilet mirrors and dressing cases was beginning to abound amongst the wealthier sections of society.

In the Boston Museum of Fine Arts, USA, is an embroidered casket of 1657 in fine tent stitch, which has a slightly tapered lid with a tray under it and two doors below opening out to disclose drawers, but this appears to have been a trinket box rather than one for embroidery. On page 17 is an illustration of an early stumpwork box dated 1693 in the possession of one of the

National Trust properties. This is an interesting example for those engaging in needlework and embroidery, not only in regard to stumpwork, but also as depicting the very 'modernistic' trend of the embroideress's mind in that the subject on the lid is 'The Judgement of Solomon' and that worthy monarch is depicted wearing Stuart dress and bearing a most striking resemblance to Charles I! Old and faded though the silks and colours of this old box now are, after nearly three hundred years, in its original state with shiny white satin, reds, pinks and blues fresh against the gold and silver and the gleaming seed pearls, it must indeed have been a thing of loveliness. The interior is divided into several small compartments at one side, offset by a larger one, presumably for holding embroidery materials, and all are padded and lined with soft sage-green silk.

THE NEEDLEWORK BOX 'ARRIVES'

Under the influence of the fine cabinet-makers and joiners of the late seventeenth and early eighteenth centuries, now working in beautiful and varied woods, and constantly seeking every possible opportunity to find new outlets for their creative skills, domestic furniture, as we know it, began to come into its own. A revolutionary change in outlook and in domestic habits had begun, and with the new ideas came the first needlework boxes in their recognisable and stylised form. It is probable, also, that they owe a good deal to the increase of traffic and commerce with India and the Far East. For centuries Eastern craftsmen had been famous for the quality of their exquisitely made caskets, but many of the earliest Indian workboxes are, purely and simply, beautiful boxes. The particular style we know today as a workbox, with its divided compartments and neat fittings for gradually more and more specialised accessories, is certainly a Western development. Once the advantages of such a portable workbox for needlework tools had been grasped, English craftsmen were swift to use their creative skills upon such items and there was no end to their ingenuity. Gradually workboxes became more and more subdivided, and had little trays which could be lifted out, pouch pockets fitted into the lids, secret compartments with special spring locks where letters could be kept, and even, in some cases, small musical boxes inserted into the base. Workboxes had at last come into their own.

The Needlework Table

It was during the latter years of the eighteenth century that the fashion for workboxes on stands, and for the needlework table, arose. The workbox on a stand was a development from the *huche* previously mentioned, but the worktable was a new idea. Usually such articles were very simple, though elegant, being fitted with only one, or at the most two, plain drawers. At this period these were not usually divided into compartments, though many had such divisions or trays added at a later date. The advantage of the worktable over the box type was that it gave a flat surface for the needlewoman to work on, or to lay her various implements on, but it did mean that she was restricted to working in one place. The workbox, which eventually gained most favour, was, on the other hand, portable—an advantage when, for instance, the owner wished to sew in the garden, or another room, or to take her embroidery work with her on holiday or on visits to friends or relatives.

At Dodington House, near Chipping Sodbury, in Gloucestershire, is a simple, elegant Sheraton worktable of rectangular octagonal shape, in warm gold mahogany, on slender tapering legs, a charming example of Sheraton at his very best. Frequently he used lyre-shaped end supports, or standards on splayed feet, but these seldom achieve the supreme elegance of his simpler styles. Another kind of worktable had a silk bag below, which contained the various silks, materials and working accessories. An early Sheraton example of this type, the property of the Earl of Ancaster, was for some time on loan to the Victoria & Albert Museum, and Sheraton's own name for this type of workbox was a 'pouch table'. The writer remembers a burred walnut worktable of this particular type, though of considerably earlier date, being of late Queen Anne period, in the home of her godmother. The green silk bag hanging below had been renewed during the early part of the nineteenth century, and at some time, probably a little before this, two separate trays had been added which were fitted with various small compartments. These are unusual in this style of worktable, since at the time of its original inception tools were still kept in small etui or pochettes and were merely dropped in on top of the embroideries deposited in the pouche.

There is an interesting needlework table in the form of a globe in the Lady Lever Art Gallery, Port Sunlight, Cheshire. The top of the globe slides back to form the lid and discloses the compartments within. A similar one was given to Princess Augusta as a birthday gift in 1810, by Queen Charlotte, and is now in Buckingham Palace.

Some of the eighteenth-century Continental worktables are very lovely and display great distinction and elegance of form. Usually they were made of walnut, mahogany, rosewood, satinwood or other woods and were decorated with marquetry, or inlaid with a variety of elaborate designs. It is not always easy to distinguish between Dutch and English worktables of this period, since influence and work intermingled. The late eighteenth-century one shown on page 18 has been influenced by Dutch design, and is of walnut with a floral marquetry pattern in vari-coloured woods, the interior being lined and fitted with deep blue silk and with ivory fittings. The reel-holders in this worktable are of particular interest, being of carved ivory and slightly convex, which is much rarer than the flat-topped type.

Materials Used in Workboxes

As with worktables, the materials used in the making of workboxes are interesting and often beautiful. Shagreen had been popular for centuries, and had been used with great skill in making the many small containers in which our ancestors delighted. But in the eighteenth and nineteenth centuries it began to go out of vogue and plain, veneered or painted woods of great variety, as in the case of worktables, began to take its place. Satinwood became fashionable in the late eighteenth century and remained so during the early 1800s. The two boxes shown on page 90 date from the latter period, but are of box or an ordinary white wood varnished over. 'Jane's Box', the larger of the two, with a painted scene on the lid, is a child's or young girl's workbox, and has a secret compartment in the bottom of it. So many workboxes have their secret compartment—nearly always held in place by a long bolt

which, when pulled up, releases a spring in the bottom of the box
which pushes the drawer out—that such compartments can hardly
ever have been as much of a secret as their owners may have fondly
believed. The French satinwood box shown on the lower part of
the same page, dates from about 1820. It is decorated with views
of Paris on its sides and top and is lined with deep pink. Lemon-
wood also began to be used in the 1800s, as did cheaper white
woods which could be painted all over, or stained and varnished to
imitate other woods such as harewood, sycamore, chestnut and
satinwood.

Another fashion which came to the fore between 1775 and 1810,
and which had a return of popularity in mid-Victorian days, was
rolled-paper work. In this, narrow strips of paper are rolled
tightly and then one edge is glued to the background panel of
wood. The tiny scrolls are packed very closely together, painted,
varnished and gilded, and formed into patterns.

Fine paper, imitating leather, ribbed velvet, shagreen and other
materials, was also used by the French to cover caskets in the latter
part of the eighteenth century, probably more as a form of craftsmanship and artistry than for reasons of economy, since the fittings
of some of these paper-covered boxes are most luxurious, being in
tortoiseshell and mother-of-pearl, and sometimes in gold or silver.

Yet another variation was straw-work needlework boxes. These
are usually of French manufacture, though many were actually
made here in England during the Napoleonic wars, by French
prisoners of war who used their hours of enforced leisure to good
profit, making many articles for sale and bringing new crafts to
England. The art of straw-work had been highly developed in
Spain, Italy, and France during the seventeenth century, but it
does not seem to have been practised in England until the later
years of the eighteenth century and only up to the early part of
Victoria's reign, when those who may have learned the art from
the French prisoners probably died out or else turned their skills
to newer fashions. Straw-work is mainly found in geometric and
floral marquetry patterns, less frequently in landscapes and figure
subjects.

By the middle of the nineteenth century, English boxes were
being made in a diversity of forms and materials which brought

them within a price range available not only to the wealthier classes, as previously, but also to most other people, so that by the end of the century they were almost *de rigueur* for all homes but the very poorest. Some of these boxes were in plain or painted woods, fitted with simple tools; some were in papiermâché, or covered with leather or velvet; but nearly always they were fitted with sets of matching implements. For the most part, they were sold in shops specialising in fancy goods, as they had been in the previous century. The well-known 'Temple of Fancy', in London, sold workboxes amongst its extraordinary range of items, including white-wood ones '. . . in a variety of shapes, for painting the inlaid ebony and ivory, and every requisite useful for painting and ornamenting the same'; and circulating libraries and stationers' shops sold designs such as classical figures, fruits, flowers and border patterns, for decorating small pieces of furniture, workboxes and the like. 'Do it yourself' was never more in vogue than during the nineteenth century.

Although perhaps not strictly belonging to this chapter, it would be a pity not to mention one particular form of needlework basket seen in the reserves at the Victoria & Albert Museum. This was made on the same principle as a double-ended umbrella. One end opens out to form a four-legged base, and the other to form a tulip-shaped receptacle which is the actual workbasket. The central wooden stem unscrews in the middle so that, when the ends are collapsed, the whole object can be folded neatly in two for storage. Both the stand and the basket top are made of alternate bands of green and white satin and trimmed with green and white silk fringing. The octagonal-shaped top has small pockets inset all round the brim, and is decorated with four long green and white cords with tasselled ends. Of late Victorian or Edwardian design, it was clearly intended as a garden workbasket, and as such was of a purely temporary nature, a plaything rather than a piece of personal equipage for serious use.

Dating the Needlework Box

The material of which a workbox is made may sometimes give a clue as to its age, for workboxes themselves, unfortunately, only rarely give any firm indication except in those cases where painting has been used to ornament the lid, when sometimes the painter's signature is attached. Some boxes, however, do bear their maker's name and indicate the reign of manufacture. Thus, for instance, if one is querying whether a particular box is Victorian or Georgian, and there is a maker's label in the lid or printed on the padding which says: 'Edwards, Manufacturers to His Majesty, 21 King Street, Bloomsbury, London', the problem is solved. But this is rare and the task of dating a box is far from easy. Many boxes have a small plate or medallion on the lid, or inside it, bearing an inscription which usually gives the donor's name and details of the recipient and the nature of the gift, and sometimes a date. This is not always quite as helpful as it might seem on first sight, since such inscriptions do not necessarily date the box, having often been added at a later period when the box was handed down, perhaps as a gift to a daughter or beloved godchild or niece.

The worktools seldom bear any maker's name, unless they are English and executed in silver or gold. Foreign silver is not always marked, and even when tools were made by a silversmith they might not be in precious metals entirely, and the amount of silver used on the mount might not be sufficient to warrant the hallmark. For instance, thimbles made between 1739 and 1790 were exempt from hallmarking, although many silversmiths continued to have them stamped. The fact that the hallmark is missing therefore does not always mean that the thimble is not silver and, if English, lack of hallmark can be of assistance in assessing its period approximately. But for the most part, tools were the work of the ordinary cutler and were not regarded as works of art, and so were unsigned.

Locks are sometimes able to give some clue in dating a box. Early plates and escutcheons are fairly easy to assess. Box locks with link plates (ie, the 'closed' type of catch as opposed to the 'hook' type) and inlaid keyhole escutcheons, usually indicate late eighteenth-century manufacture. Initially they were often hand-sawn from the metal plate, but later on were cast, and finally degenerated into stamped fittings. Handles also may be helpful, in so far as they tend to follow the furniture styles of the period. The strongly rococo styles of the mid-1700s, and the simpler types of the ensuing classical reversion in the next twenty years or so, often help place a box whose date is otherwise indeterminate. The popular lions' heads gripping rings in their mouths came in with the last year or two of the eighteenth century and remained firm favourites for a considerable time, but from late Georgian times onwards it is unwise to pontificate too firmly on datings. Heavy rococo mounts, neo-Gothic, neo-classical, novel, even gimmicky types may all be found (usually distracting from the lines of the box itself) but the finest, and those which give most lasting pleasure, are nearly always those which relied upon clean lines, simplicity in both design and decoration, and the gracious beauty of fine polished woods to enhance their effect.

Examples of Workboxes and Fittings

In late eighteenth-century boxes, writing implements are frequently found combined with needlework tools, and from the middle of the following century the Victorian passion for dual-purpose efficiency asserted itself in this direction also, so that they, too, frequently fitted their boxes with both sets of implements. Ink bottles, pounce pots, small penknives for sharpening quills or pencils, and rulers, are all found rubbing shoulders with the fitted mounts containing scissors, stilettos, crochet hooks, bodkins and needlecases. But somehow most of these boxes seem to lack character and the collector's taste will usually incline towards the straightforward needlework box.

During the early years of the nineteenth century the vogue arose for using miniature pieces of furniture as sewing cabinets. These were often 'salesman's samples', taken round as examples of styles of work, and which eventually became popular as household pieces and were sometimes fitted with compartments for specific tools; but these miniature cabinets and chests of drawers never had the popularity of the true workbox. There are also the travelling-cases which were taken when journeying, and these again were usually in the form of small cabinets or chest of drawers, as had been such earlier compendiums, but with each drawer being fitted for its specific purpose. Thus the top drawer might be for embroidery tools, the next for writing materials, the next for jewellery, and the lowest one for oddments. These again can hardly be classed as true needlework boxes, but are interesting as exemplifying the efficiency and practicality of the Victorian mind.

The most usual implements included in the fittings of a workbox were, initially, a pair of scissors, a needlecase, thimble, bodkins, and a stiletto. To these were sometimes added a couple of pairs of knitting needles and a crochet hook. In the small compartments intended for cottons, there were either cotton barrels or reel-holders, according to the age and style of the box. These are more fully dealt with in a later chapter but are mentioned here in order that the average contents of a fitted case may be envisaged. The needlework box shown on page 18 is a typical early nineteenth-century example, being of about 1810. It came from the Isambard Owen family of Glyn Melyn, Abersoch, and is now in the Welsh Folk Museum (National Museum of Wales) at St Fagans.

In most of these boxes the style is fairly constant. There is usually a hinged flap in the lid, which opens out to form a small pocket or pouch, in which small pieces of work could be kept. Some of these have a secret lock, but most have a simple stay which keeps the flap in place. In many a small mirror is inserted into the lid. The tray is divided into a number of small compartments, and lifts out to reveal a lower compartment to hold larger items and pieces of material. The diagram on page 30 shows the positioning of the compartments in the tray, and is a typical example of the style used in the more elaborately fitted caskets, the less expensive ones having fewer divisions, and often with only half of the upper compartment forming a tray.

Many boxes were fitted for more specialised types of work, as in the case of the black lacquer Chinese workbox of c 1840 (plate, page 36) which is fitted with a rachet and netting spool, netting needles and pins, and tatting shuttles, as well as the ordinary cotton barrels and multiple cotton winders. In the right-hand compartment above the small painted rectangular lid is an ivory needlecase, and in the matching compartment on the other side is a crochet handle containing a set of hooks. There were also boxes especially fitted for the type of work known as pillow lace. In the Victoria & Albert Museum there is a workbox which is interesting as another example of a case with special fitments. This is English, nineteenth-century, probably c 1830, and is made of wood covered

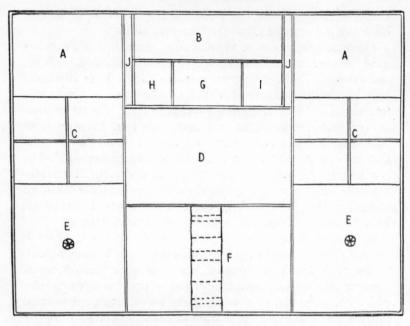

2 *Diagram of typical workbox interior and fittings*

A—*Pin-cushion, silk or velvet covered*
B— *Compartments for small tools, shuttles, needlecase, etc*
C—*Compartments for cotton barrels, reel-holders, etc*
D—*Open compartment for small accessories*
E— *Compartments fitted with lids in silk or velvet, with small handles for lifting*
F— *Compartment covered by pad with narrow band slotted to take scissors, bodkins and other tools*
G—*Thread waxer, emery or wax-holder, etc*
H—*Thimble*
I— *Space for tape measure or finger shield*
J— *Fitted needlecases in matching silk or velvet*

with shagreen and lined with pale blue satin. It contains two ivory winders and four small circular ivory boxes which held spools of gold and silver thread. Another one in the same museum, similar in covering and lining and of the same period, contains a circular box of turned ivory and tortoiseshell, which holds seven small, numbered boxes, also of turned ivory, each one holding different types of sequins, spangles, bugles and other beads for embroidery. Numbered boxes like this must have been particularly useful when working with the tiny, multi-coloured, variously shaped beads used in the beadwork so fashionable during the Victorian era.

A style very popular in the early 1800s, and usually of French or Italian origin, was the workbox in the shape of a spinet. An example, now in the National Museum of Wales, is illustrated on page 54. When the lid is lifted it reveals an inset mirror and a very lovely set of sewing tools set in purple velvet decorated with fine beadwork. Most of these spinet-type boxes have a musical box fitted in the 'keyboard' end—in this case, under the velvet and silver-bead encrusted pincushion which can be seen in the photograph. The fittings are of silver, elaborately chased and ornamented, and consist of a silver-stoppered glass scent bottle, a pair of silver handled scissors, two mother-of-pearl spool holders, a silver-handled stiletto, and a silver needlecase and matching bodkin case containing a silver thimble and bodkin. It must have been a gift calculated to win any lady's heart, and still brings a gleam to a collector's eye today. Similar examples are believed to have been made in the shape of a harp, but the writer has never as yet come across one, and they were probably never quite so popular as the spinet style.

As has been mentioned earlier, during the late eighteenth and early and mid-nineteenth centuries, the skill of the Indian box-makers was diverted into the production of workboxes to suit the European taste. The range and variety is wide. There are caskets of ivory, either turned, carved, or plain; sandalwood and cedarwood boxes of the finest tracery and carving; lacquered boxes and coffers; tortoiseshell boxes; and caskets beautifully inlaid with mother-of-pearl, ebony and other materials. The one illustrated on page 35 is a fine example of the heights which were achieved by some of these craftsmen. It was commissioned by Sir Ralph Palmer, Chief Justice of Madras, about 1828, as an engagement gift for his niece, Mrs Elizabeth Biddulph, *née* Palmer. More than a hundred years later, in 1940, it was given to her great granddaughter, Mrs Elizabeth Sowdon, who still has it. It is made of ivory inlaid with ebony and lined with cedarwood. The slightly pagoda-shaped lid of the casket itself is made of single tusks all tapering to a central point, and the sides of the box are composed of perfectly matched pieces of tusk laid side by side in palisade fashion. The interior is fitted with compartments lined with either red velvet or with cedarwood, with an array of needlework tools fitted into the centre section. There is a small recessed panel in the lid, fitted with a key, and surrounded by a border of mosaic in ebony. The lids to the various compartments are made of ivory, as are the various spool-holders and boxes with which it is fitted. In the illustration, some of the contents may be seen beside the box.

There are still a number of such Eastern boxes to be found, but whilst it is true to say that the finest examples are fashioned throughout with great delicacy and precision, there are also many where the actual tools themselves are of poor workmanship. The difference probably lies between those boxes which were especially commissioned and were therefore fashioned by the very finest craftsmen available, and those which were made for the not inconsiderable European market represented by the ever-increasing number of European visitors and the sailors who called at the great Indian ports. For the most part, the native craftsman had little conception as to the use to which the various tools were to be put, and no particular training in their construction. On the other hand, behind him lay a very long tradition and an exacting apprenticeship in the actual making of fine boxes and caskets, so that part of his work would be excellent, and part inclined to be faulty. Many of the purchasers also, being men, would not have known exactly what to look for in the various implements. To their eyes they were probably exactly like those they remembered having seen in England, and they did not notice or appreciate the flaws and omissions in many of them. But the purchaser who had ordered a special casket probably took pains to ensure that the workman fulfilling his commission knew exactly what tools were required, and made sure that they were executed to perfection.

The other Indian workbox (shown on page 71) and which is now in the Welsh Folk Museum, is less elaborate and has no tools fitted. Nevertheless, it has a beauty of its own. Made of sandalwood, the lid and sides are carved with oriental scenes, depicting the elephant-headed god Ganeshe on his rat-mount, Narada the patron of music, and Vishna, all set amidst panels of exotic foliage and flowers. The lid lifts off to reveal a tray of nine loose-lidded compartments, with ivory knobs for handles, and two small open compartments. There are no fitted tools and, in fact, these lidded compartment types very seldom have any fitments in them. This box was given in 1854 to Maria Russell, later wife of Arthur Charles Humphreys-Owen of Glansevern. The recipient's delight in her gift is described on page 151.

There is an interesting example of the different interpretation which may be put upon fitments in a workbox in the American Museum at Bath (plate, page 72). This is a birdseye-maple sewing-box of 1791 which belonged to Mrs Benedict Arnold, wife of the American traitor, General Benedict Arnold, of the War of Independence. It was made by Elasaba, a Micmac Indian woman, and is a beautiful example of fine Indian work in the shaping of the little birchwood caskets and boxes, combined with an astonishing appreciation of 'English' style embroidery in the delicate sprays of flowers, grapes and other items which Elasaba worked on the covers of the boxes. The story of this workbox and its owner is related in Chapter 9.

It may be of interest here to remark on a special and unusual type of American workbox, known as the 'Shaker' box, one of which can be seen on page 72. These were made and used by the religious sect known as Shakers, and are simply formed of maple-wood. The Shakers were extremely puritanical and austere in their whole way of life, having nothing about them which was not essential and living by the motto 'Hands to work, and hearts to God', so that all their work was done with utmost perfection and care, and every moment of their time disciplined and strictly accounted for. These boxes were kept on the bench or table at which the Shakers worked, and all work was put away immediately into the boxes as soon as the working period was over. The boxes are beautifully formed and fashioned and never contained anything more than the most essential tools and the work immediately in hand. Not for the Shakers the many intriguing divisions and compartments of their more sophisticated sisters' workboxes!

The wooden casket shown on page 17 is a typical English box of c 1830 and now in the National Museum of Wales. It is in coffer-style, with a raised lid, and is carved and inlaid. Inside, it is lined with dark royal-blue silk, and the double-flapped pocket in the lid has a gilt, tooled-leather surround. The tray is also lined with royal-blue silk and was originally fitted with mother-of-pearl accessories. Such boxes are so frequently lined with pale pastel-coloured silks that this one makes a charming and refreshing change.

There is another casket in the American Museum at Bath, which is an interesting example of brass scrollwork on velvet. The interior is lined with pale cream satin and velvet, and fitted with finely chased tools including six cotton spool-holders, a ruler, penknife, bodkin, stiletto, needle, tambour hook, pencil, yard measure, needlecase and silver thimble.

OTHER TYPES OF CONTAINERS

Flat Sewing Cases

From the seventeenth to the nineteenth centuries, the flat cases holding a few essential needlework tools, which were a continuation of the sewing-purse or wallet and could be carried in a bag or pocket, continued to be made. A pleasant early example of this style of sewing case may be seen on page 89. It is of polished wood, and fitted with purple velvet. The tools, which include a needlecase, scissors, and seam-presser and stiletto combined, are refreshingly simple in their slightly severe, almost puritanical lines, and make a welcome relief from the more ornate implements which are so often found. It is believed to date from the early days of the eighteenth century or the end of the previous century, and the tools are of polished steel. Cases of this type were made in ivory, various polished woods, shagreen and velvet.

Etuis and Chatelaines

It has already been mentioned that something like the etui and chatelaine existed in Anglo-Saxon and medieval times and lasted, in a simplified version, right into our own day—there is a drawing of an eighteenth-century etui on page 37. In richly decorated forms it had been very popular during the seventeenth and eighteenth centuries, and by the end of the latter we find extremely beautiful and elaborate examples existing. Sometimes

Page 35 (above) *Indian workbox c 1828. The sides are formed from lengths of solid ivory and the lid tapers to a fluted finial knob; (below) the interior, lined with cedarwood and ivory and ebony inlay, and with red silk, with a small, locking compartment in lid. The ivory fittings comprise crochet hooks, a bodkin and stilettos, a multiple winder, two reel-holders, a silver thimble and yard measure in the shape of an acorn*

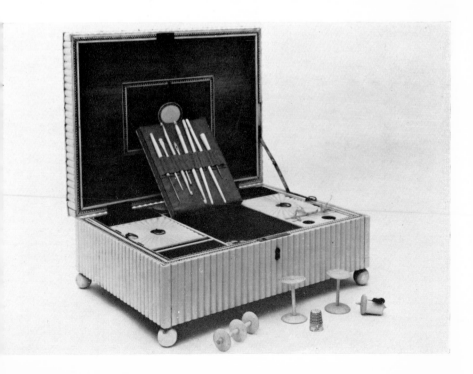

Page 36 (above) *Chinese lacquered needlework box, with gilt claw feet and drop handles, c 1840; (below) the interior, with four ivory cotton barrels, netting roller and ratchet. Below; a tambour handle and needlecase with netting needles, gauge and pins in centre, and ivory shuttle and multiple winder. At the bottom, a thread-waxer, small spool, winding spool and thimble*

they are called etui, and sometimes necessaire, but the word etui seems to be more usual today, and necessaire usually referred more to an article of a box-like shape and character, as the one shown (plate, page 54) which is in the State Historical Museum, Moscow.

3 *Etui case, c 1760, closed; and with lid open*

Many etui are in silver or in gold, richly chased with fruit and foliage and classical scenes, and often studded with pearls and precious stones. Others are in fine enamels, and nearly all are upright, slightly cylindrical, or becoming gradually flatter in form as they increase in complexity of contents. They are some 4 to 5in high. They contained not only sewing implements, such as needles, a bodkin, folding scissors and sometimes a thimble, but also such other items as a penknife, or a tiny fruitknife, a buttonhook, a pen, and quite often a compass. All manner of fitments were gradually added into these very beautiful little cases, all screwing into elegant handles of silver-gilt, gold, mother-of-pearl and other fine materials; but the oldest forms were intended mainly for sewing implements and developed from the old medieval needlecase. There are a number of very fine etuis of the eighteenth century in the Albert & Victoria Museum in London, belonging to Dr Joan Evans's collection, and although the average collector may seldom have the opportunity of finding such rare specimens as these today, it is nevertheless well worth seeing such items whenever possible. There are also a number of very interesting chatelaines in the same collection and belonging to the same period. All are made of pinchbeck, richly ornamented and chased, and several amongst them are enamelled. Illustrated on page 107, is a Russian sixteenth-century chatelaine from the State Historical Museum, Moscow.

The main difference between a chatelaine and an etui is that the chatelaine was a large clasp or hook which fitted on to the belt, and from which depended several chains or rings, each supporting separate items such as scissors, penknife, needlecase and other objects as desired, whereas the etui is a single container with a variety of items all neatly fitting into it, and usually carried in a purse or pocket. Only very occasionally would an etui be carried suspended from the waist and it is very rare, in fact, to find them with a ring or hook for suspension, though sometimes there are small side chains attached to them and quite often a safety chain fastening the lid to the main body of the etui. Many of the more elaborately decorated ones were indeed more by way of being ornaments than anything else, and often stood on a small table, or in a desk or needlework case. The chatelaine, on the other hand, was always worn on the person. Although sometimes found in a workbox, strictly speaking neither of them belong among the fittings, both being, virtually, miniature needlework holders in their own right. It is quite incorrect to use the terms as though they were alternative forms for the same article, as is sometimes done in modern sale catalogues. They are two quite separate articles.

With the slim dresses of the Empire and Regency periods, the chatelaine went out of fashion. But towards the mid-1800s, the return of fuller skirts and the advent of the Romantic era with its legends of King Arthur and his knights, brought in a revival of interest in medieval castles and the life and dress of a highly glamourised medieval way of life. It became fashionable to wear a chatelaine once more, and many a mid-Victorian housewife had her bunch of keys and other small necessaries hanging from the waist. But over and beyond such a purely domestic and utilitarian purpose, the vogue also set in again for chatelaines which consisted solely of sewing implements. These were by no means as beautiful or as elegant as those of the days immediately preceding the French Revolution. They are usually much heavier in design, and were probably worn far more for effect, for playing 'the charming custodian of the fairy castle' of the Arthurian cycle, than for service, since by now the workbox with its fitted tools was the established place to which a woman would resort for her sewing, rather than to the objects hanging from her waist, except perhaps for immediate emergency repairs on occasion.

THE DECLINE OF THE WORKBOX

By Edwardian times the heyday of the needlework box was nearly over. The Victorian pendulum had swung too far and too heavily now, and it was on its downward return. Emancipation was in the air, and young ladies no longer spent hours in their drawing-rooms working at their frames or their tatting and crochet. The sewing machine, too, had made its mark, and not only could it do plain sewing twice as quickly as any seamstress, but it could even engage in various simple, but fairly spectacular, types of embroidery, with or without a frame. Young ladies were no longer expected to regard fine stitchery as an indispensible part of their education, and most of them made it quite clear that they intended to limit their activities in that sphere to essential repairs to their personal clothing, and little else! More time for leisure brought sport and travel into prominence, and the quiet Victorian evenings doing sewing and embroidery whilst Papa read an improving book aloud, were past. The elegant, highly polished workboxes belonging to Mama and Grandmama were beginning to take on the air of museum pieces as they stood, neglected, on the sofa tables and bureaus. For a younger, restless, swift-moving generation they were too cumbersome, too full of too many compartments and gadgets. Things needed to be simple, easy to find, easy to work, less fussy than the intracacies of the needlework box and its trays and tiny compartments. Lidded wickerwork baskets, either circular or rectangular, with lined and padded interiors were gradually taking their place, and are still in fairly common use today. Indeed, the total span of life of the workbox in the form we are discussing is only a little more than 200 years, so far as collectors are concerned; yet (as is shown in Chapter 10) within that short space of time a wide variety of types is available, and it is still possible to find interesting, and even unusual, items in house sales and at other auctions, their original contents and jumble of odds and ends still awaiting a careful sifting through, and very frequently revealing a wealth of unsuspected Victoriana. But in many of them the original fitments have been lost, broken, or so jumbled about that a novice may have little or no idea as to what each item represents, and its purpose, or what is needed to replace the missing pieces in the various compartments.

It is with the various types of fitted contents, and also with the surprising oddments contained in many old sewing-boxes, that the next few chapters deal, in the hope that collectors will be able to fit out their boxes in something akin to their original state, and perhaps also to branch out to collect individual items and sets.

CHAPTER 2

THE COMMON PIN

See that there be not a loose pin in the work of your salvation

So wrote the great Scottish divine, Rutherford, in a letter to a friend in 1637, and one wonders which type of pin he had in mind, since they are used in so many and such differing trades, from sewing and weaving to metal work.

According to the learned Dr Johnson, the origin of the word 'pin' is the Latin word *spina*, meaning a thorn. Other authorities, however, advance the Anglo-Saxon verb *pyndan*, meaning to pin, pen, or pound. Each to his choice, but we find Chaucer in the fourteenth century spelling the word as though from its Anglo-Saxon derivation—'Thy pleasant laune pinned with golden pene' —and early writers speak of the 'pinner', or 'pindar', as one whose task it was to pin, or pen, the sheep into the pinfold or penfold. Some old writers also speak of 'drinking a merry pin', and the phrase would be unintelligible to us today if we did not know of an old custom which entailed fixing pins, or pegs, into a drinking-cup to measure the depth of draught the guest was expected to achieve. The origin of the word 'pinafore', or 'pin-before', comes from the custom of pinning a cloth, or pinner, across the breast to save the dress during meals, and was of course especially applicable to children; in time it became a permanent article of clothing, being finally attached by strings rather than pins, but retaining its original name. Probably both root-words combined to form the final form, *spina* indicating the thornlike spike, and *pyndan* the use to which it was put, of folding, fixing, keeping in place. In Scottish dialect the word for a pin is *prein*, the smallest pin being called a minikin prein, and the largest a bodle prein.

41

The very earliest pins are indeed likely to have been long prick-thorns such as are used even today in primitive tribes. Contemporary with, or perhaps slightly later, and probably depending a good deal on climatic conditions, came bone pins. The thorn type did, in fact, continue in use right down to Elizabethan times, as seventeenth-century literature mentions in several places and, even in our own day, witches are still in the habit of using thornpins rather than the more usual type of pin or nail, when they affix sheep's hearts or other even more nauseous objects to doors and posts. There may be a ritual reason for this, but it is an interesting insight into the continuance of very old practices. Through all centuries both thorns and the later pins have been used in the unpleasant witchcraft practice of inserting pins into a waxen image or doll, with the intent to harm or destroy the person whom the image represents.

The simplest bone pins are little more than skewers, as may be seen from the Neolithic type illustrated on page 43, which comes from the Tŷ-isaf long cairn at Brecknock, and dates from c 2500 BC. Moving later in time, there are a large number of Roman pins in Britain, and they are in fact amongst some of the more common articles found during archaeological searches. Most of those discovered in Britain are of bone or bronze, though quite a number have been found in ivory, jet, silver, iron and glass. They are seldom less than 2½in long and not often more than 6in at the most. The simpler types are still skewer-like, being of bone or ivory, and having poorly formed or no heads at all. But by far the majority have been turned in the lathe, with a wide variety of head shapings, as may be seen on page 44. In the more elaborate forms, the heads are carved with decorative terminals in the form of birds, animals, busts and tiny statuettes, whilst some amongst the bronze pins have been enamelled. These ornamental pins were probably used for pinning garments.

Besides being used for sewing purposes and for fastening the dress, pins were also used to pin the hair, but there seems to be no special feature distinguishing their different uses. In all probability they were used indiscriminately, although some sort of differentiation may be concluded by presuming that the bronze ones were used for dress and sewing, and the larger, broader ones of jet, ivory and bone, were for the hair. The growth of the pin into the hairpin, haircomb and hair ornaments is dealt with on page 50. Of the bronze pins, the smaller types were probably used for sewing purposes and the slightly larger types for fastening robes with either a utilitarian or a decorative intent.

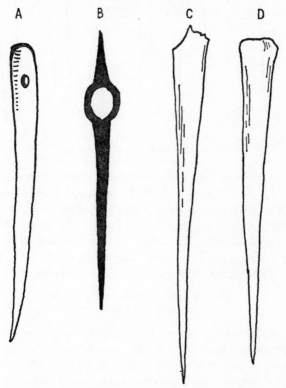

4 *Bone and bronze needles 1000 BC and 300 BC and pins c 2500 BC*
    A—Polished bone needle, c 1000 BC
    B— Bronze needle, early Iron Age, c 300 BC
    C—Broken pin or needle of bone, c 2500 BC
    D—Neolithic pin c 2500 BC
       (In National Museum of Wales, Cardiff)

Wooden pins, or skewers, were still the normal type used in medieval times, and even as late as the reign of Elizabeth I,

5 *Roman bone and ivory pins with plain and turned heads*
(In National Museum of Wales, Cardiff)

wooden skewers or pins were considered essential articles of the
toilet table. Metal pins were still comparatively rare and quite
costly. Along with the manufacture of needles, which is touched
on briefly in the next chapter, we believe the monasteries also
made pins, since there are various allusions to this in literature.
Chaucer's oft-quoted lines describing the friar in *The Canterbury
Tales* are amongst the best known of all pin-references:

> His typet was ay stuffed full of knyves
> And pyns for to give to faire wyves.

But, on the whole, pinmaking as an industry was practically
non-existent in this country. There was a Company of Pinmakers,
or Pinners, as early as 1376, when records show that they returned
two men to the Common Council of London. In 1469 they were
responsible for twenty men for the City Watch, but they do not
seem to have been a very powerful body. Since they were linked to
the Wiredrawers, it is probable that their main strength came
from that side of the Company. It is not until 1543 that we find an
Act passed by Henry VIII to encourage the manufacture of good
pins—just possibly the dissolution of the monasteries had something to do with the matter, since it must have become more
urgent to re-establish centres of pinmaking now that the monks

were no longer able to take part in their manufacture. Previously France had been the main centre for pinmaking, and Paris in particular, though attempts had been made in England to extend the industry, and in 1483 a statute had been passed to prohibit the importation of pins into England. This seems to have been singularly ineffectual, and was obviously disregarded since Catharine Howard is said to have preferred French pins for her royal toilet, as being of a far greater fineness and accuracy than those made here.

Because of their price, pins were mainly available only to the wealthier sections of society, and we know that they were acceptable as New Year gifts to ladies, and also that special presents of money were given for the sole purpose of purchasing pins, regarded as indispensable for any gentlewoman's toilet requirements. The term 'pin money', in fact, derives from the custom between merchants of concluding any financial transaction with a small sum of money for the merchant's wife, 'for her pynns'.

Under the Act passed by Henry VIII, pins were only allowed to be sold on two days in the year, on 1 and 2 January. In the same Act, the manner of manufacture was also stipulated: '. . . no person shall put to the sale any pin, but only such as shall be double-headed, and have the heads soldered fast to the shanks of the pin, well-smoothed, the shanks well shapen, the points well and round filed, canted and sharpened. . . .' Once the pin industry had become established in England, however, it went ahead with astonishing swiftness, and by 1650 we find Ralph Verney writing home from France for English or 'proper pinns' to be sent to his wife, since 'they are nought here'.

In the years following the Reformation, Gloucester became the great centre of the pin trade, though the first written evidence of pinmaking there is in 1608, when John Payter in West Ward, and Thomas Edge in St Nicholas Parish, were noted as 'pinners' (*Man and Armour for Gloucestershire*, by John Smith of Nibley). Their pins were probably put to sterner use than merely emergency repairs for ladies' gowns or the gentler arts of sewing and embroidery since, in this context, 'pinners' usually refers to those making the rivets, or pins, for suits of armour.

In 1626 the mayor and burgesses of Gloucester provided one John Tilsley, of Bristol, with a rent-free house in which he could start a factory for the making of pins. This circumstance is referred to in one of Dibdin's songs:

> The ladies, Heaven bless them all,
> As sure as I've a nose on,
> In former times had only thorns
> And skewers to stick their clothes on
> No damsel then was worth a pin,
> Whate'er it might have cost her,
> Till gentle Johnny Tilsley
> Invented pins in Gloucester!

The 'invented' part is not strictly accurate, but Dibdin's verses—he lived from 1745–1814—are often very topical, and we know from old records that pinmaking had, by 1744, become the city's chief industry.

Tilsley's venture prospered, and proved to the whole county's benefit, since the work spread and formed a cottage industry as far out as Berkeley and Dursley. By 1802 there were nine factories employing 1,500 people out of a total estimated population of 7,600; but after 1824, when an automatic machine was patented for the making of solid-headed pins, decline set in and the centre of the industry moved to Birmingham. By 1838 there were only three pin factories left in Gloucester, and by 1867 only one.

Incidentally, the 'gentle Johnny Tilsley' of the poem shows how a man's attributes live on in the public memory, for John Tilsley really was a good and compassionate man. Seeing how many orphans and poor children ran about the streets with neither shelter nor prospects, Tilsley had the idea of employing them and teaching them the trade of pinmaking. When Bristol Corporation lent him £100 and the house in which to set up his factory, he took seventy children from the orphanages and set them to work in what were then very good conditions. They lived together and had proper food and adequate clothing; because of the dust from the pins it was necessary to have good ventilation in the factory, and also good lighting so that the finer and smaller pins could be easily seen. Thus they had companionship, very favourable working conditions, the opportunity to learn a trade and, eventually, if they desired, to become master-pinners and set up on their own. It is believed that in Bristol his factory mainly manufactured the old, iron pins until he made the move to Gloucester, and was able to combine the local skills there with the availability of the new brass wire being manufactured in the Midlands.

It is possible to tell old, handmade pins from the more modern types because of the different method of manufacture. Old pins always have slightly rounded, nodular heads, and are made in two pieces, the head being fitted to the shank. The modern type made by machine only began to be made about 1800 and it was not until 1830 or so that pinmaking in general began to be fully mechanised and the normally flat-headed, single-pieced pin we know today was born. Collectors will want to recognise the difference between the two types in order to furnish their boxes appropriately, so a brief account follows of the process by which handmade pins were produced.

The first requisite in the manufacture of pins is brass wire. It was owing to the lack of this commodity that the pin trade had not commenced earlier in England. Once a brass foundry was started in Birmingham and was able to supply London, Coventry and Gloucester with this essential material, there was no waste of time in starting up the industry in earnest. Since it had its own wiredrawers and 'pinners', Gloucester was in a particularly favour-able position, and Tilsley showed great acumen in seizing upon such an advantageous opportunity to use skilled men in the training of his young employees.

The making of brass wire from compounds of copper and zinc, and the rolling into sheets, or drawing into wire, was not the province of the pinmaker. His work began with the cleaning of the rough-drawn wire, by pickling it in a mixture of sulphuric acid and water. After this, it was reduced to the proper gauge by passing through a draw plate, in much the same way as in the manufacture of needles, as we shall see in the next chapter. In the case of pins, however, the operation was easier because of the greater softness of the brass wire. In the draw plate the wire was passed through various holes diminishing in size, until the different thicknesses required were achieved, varying from thick to almost hair fine. Thereafter the wire had to be straightened by zigzagging between metal pegs until all the coil or twist was taken out. It was then cut into short lengths containing enough material to make six pins. Both ends of this strip were pointed by a milling machine, and then the two end pieces were cut off at the approximate length needed, the intermediate portions being returned to the pointer and the process repeated until finally six separate, pointed, pinshafts were formed. The long, coiled heading-wire had meanwhile been cut into small 'heads', consisting of three spirals each. The pinshafts and heads were given to a young girl who whisked up one head to each shaft and then placed the latter in a small die in a heading machine, which she operated by a treadle. Once this was depressed a heavy weight suspended by a cord was lifted, and when she took her foot off the treadle the 'thumper' descended on the top of the pin, moulding the head into the distinctive shape and at the same time fastening it securely to the shaft. A really deft workwoman could head up to 1,500 pins an hour, or from 12,000 to 15,000 in a day. One of these early heading-machines can be seen in the Folk Museum at Gloucester.

The shape was now completed, but the appearance would never have justified the saying 'as bright as a new pin'; three further processes were necessary. Firstly, the pins had to be scoured or 'yellowed' for about half an hour in a solution of tartar in a hand-turned barrel: secondly, they were washed or 'whitened' in water. For this they were put in a large copper pan together with bran, and this was then filled with water and placed on the fire. When hot, cream of tartar was added and the water allowed to boil for an hour. The third process was when the pins were taken out, washed in water and dried and polished by being tossed and winnowed in warm bran. 'Mourning pins' were coated with black varnish in the earliest types, after the 'yellowing' process, but by 1850 it was usual to make them in steel wire tempered to a deep purple. This ensured that they were neater, stronger and sharper than the older, blacked, or japanned pins. For our particular purpose it also makes it easier to distinguish the age of the pin.

This completed the extraordinary complex process of manufacture, and all that remained was to fix the pins into the little crimped pin-papers in which they would be sold. These papers were crimped with irons, and the folds gathered together and held between the jaws of a vice. The workwoman drew the pins together towards her with a horn comb which held the heads between its teeth, and then, with a dextrous flicking movement of the thumb (which was shielded by a leather guard), she drove the pins through the perforated grooves of the paper.

The variety in length and thickness of these old handmade pins is almost unbelievable. The larger ones, for heavy blankets, furnishings, etc, were some 3in long and about ⅛in thick; ordinary pins were just over 1in long; and the very small 'Lilliput' types were ⅜in long and as fine in comparison. It takes 300,000 of the last mentioned to weigh one pound!

In 1824 a Mr Lemuel Wellman Wright, of the United States, patented a machine which produced 40 to 50 pins per minute. The difference between pins produced by this method and earlier pins can be seen in the head, which was forced up and formed in one movement whilst the wire was soft. Though quicker, it also meant that the pins tended to bend more in use than had the old handmade sort.

An interesting 'find' in old boxes are the wax-headed pins with which careful ladies of the early nineteenth century often supplied themselves. These seem to have been made from pins from which the head had become dislodged, or even from needles where the eye had been broken. A drop of sealing wax deposited on the head of the shaft was carefully moulded into a little knob, giving a new lease of life to the damaged article and displaying a nice sense of thrift.

By the middle of the nineteenth century one of the great pin-making firms, Messrs Kirby, Beard & Co, who had moved from Gloucester to Birmingham, were using more than 100 tons of copper and zinc annually for their trade. With their extraordinary love of aids to visualisation, Victorian writers tell us that were this quantity of metal to be converted into the tiny ribbon pins, it would produce 67,200,000,000 or about 66 to each of the then inhabitants of the globe. If placed in a straight line the pins would stretch out 525,000 miles, sufficient to reach nearly twenty-two times round the world, or more than twice the distance of the moon from the earth. The obvious question is what became of all these pins? Fortunately, old pins can still be found, with or without their pin-papers, in old boxes, drawers, under floorboards, etc, waiting only to be recognised and put into their appropriate place in workbox, hussif, or pincushion.

From being a costly handmade article, the pin became so cheap by the middle of the eighteenth century as to promote the saying 'not worth a pin', denoting something almost valueless. It is interesting to know that an eighteenth-century writer disliked the term 'pin money', and would rather that 'they had called it needle money, which might have implied something of good housewifery, and not have given the malicious world occasion to think that dress and trifles have always the uppermost place in a woman's thoughts'.

From the utilitarian sewing pin, we turn to the pin in its more decorative form; for it is one of those quirks of human behaviour that, amongst the various oddments frequently found in old needlework boxes, are hairpins, ornamental haircombs, and hair ornaments in general. Even in modern worktables it is quite common to find a packet of hairgrips slipped in beside the array of true sewing requisites.

As already noted, the earliest pins in Greek and Roman times were dual-purpose articles, used indiscriminately to pin either materials, dresses, or hair. In York Museum there are two plaster casts which are good examples of the latter usage. In one, the lady's hair is plaited and made into a coil at the back of the neck, and held in position with two jet pins. In the other, there are three jet hairpins, two of them quite small, but the third nearly 7in long and having an eye near the point. In this style—obviously a later development from the early pin, and akin to the bodkin of later years—a fine cord was fitted through the eye, then drawn over the hair and caught under the coil and tied, thus effectively securing the latter in position. Similar pins have been found elsewhere and in Apt, in the South of France, there is a marble carving of a female head showing the plaited and coiled style of headdress held in position by just such a pin. This style can be dated to about the third or fourth centuries AD, and is probably a change brought about by Christian influence from the previous over-elaborate and extravagant hair styles of the Imperial Age. Both St

Paul and the writer of the Epistles of Peter express stern disapproval of these frivolous fashions, and encourage simplicity in dress and behaviour, and in many parts of Italy, France and Germany, the plain but becoming style of the Apt headdress was still in common usage during the early years of this century.

Jet, bone, and ivory seem to have been the most popular materials for pins for the hair, probably on account of their light weight, and the entasis, or slight convexity in shape, anticipates the advantages of the later double-pronged hairpins and the curved and 'falcon' types, with their firmer hold.

Haircombs (diagram, page 52) seem to have developed side by side with pins, and from recent burial finds in Jutland we have beautiful examples of horn combs which are more than 3,000 years old and yet as perfect in form and design as many made today. From the late Dark Ages, c 800 AD we have examples such as those found at Draethen, in Glamorganshire. Here the upturned ends denote the Scandinavian influence. Combs were used not only to comb the hair but, as with the pin, to hold it in place. The Norsemen, for instance, smeared their hair thickly with fat (which, we learn, was frequently rancid and high-smelling) and then wound it up into place and secured it by combs.

Through the centuries, combs for ornamental purposes increased in height, variety and richness. By the eighteenth century they were often extremely extravagent in both material and style, though many are exquisite works of craftsmanship. By the nineteenth century they had become more restrained, and were usually of tortoiseshell, horn, or ivory, decorated with pastes, coloured glass, coral, carving or other ornamentation. They are a field of their own for collectors, with an interesting history and a wide range of styles, and they would appear to be completely out of place in this book, except for the fact that many are still to be found tucked away in the bottom of old needlework boxes. The writer can only advance as a possible reason for this that, whilst relaxing and doing her sewing, a woman may have let her hair down literally, or at least taken the weight off her head, by removing the ornamental comb she might be wearing, and dropping it into her workbox for immediate tidiness. It would appear that quite a few remained there permanently, in with all the other strange little odds and ends so often found. It seems a reasonable possibility, and certainly the person who decided to collect decorative haircombs and hair ornaments should always make a point of checking up on old needlework boxes.

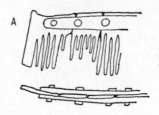

A—*The Draethen Comb, c 800 AD*
B—*Horn comb from Jutland, c 2000 BC*
(*In National Museum of Wales, Cardiff*)

Page 53 (above) *Regency needlework box, writing-case drawer under; black lacquer, decorated with mother-of-pearl and painted floral and pictorial designs. Chinese carved ivory netting case beside it is probably early 19th century; (below) small turtleshell box approx 5in × 2in, containing silver yard measure, thread-waxer, emery, thimble, bodkin and earspoon. 19th century*

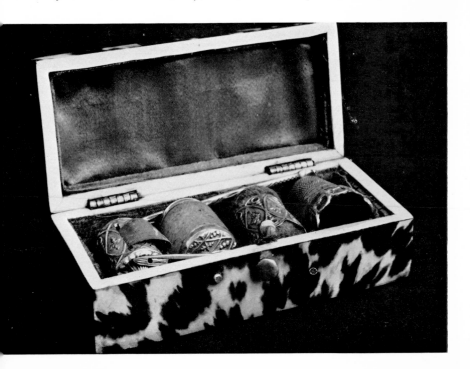

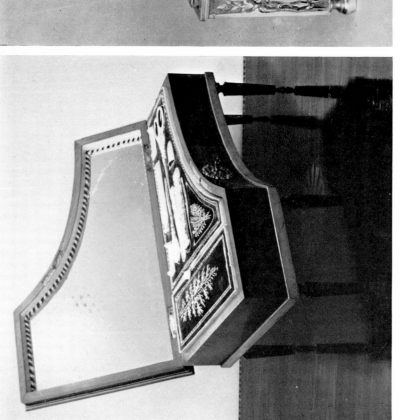

Page 54 (left) Spinet needlework box, probably French, c 1800. The tools are silver and a musical box is fitted under the pincushion; (right) English 18th-century necessaire in the shape of a small chest, framed in gold and containing a variety of sewing tools, including thimble, scissors, bodkins, needles, pincushion and pincase

CHAPTER 3

SEWING NEEDLES AND BODKINS

Man for the field and woman for the hearth:
Man for the sword and for the needle she . . .
Tennyson, *The Princess*

SEWING NEEDLES

Such an essential tool as a needle must have a long history, and certainly needles were used in Neolithic times; primitive man fashioned his rough clothes and few furnishings and covering with the simplest of all possible needle forms—a sharp pointed animal or fish bone, pierced at one end with a hole. Whether the article in the diagram on page 43 is a pin or needle can never now be ascertained; it could be either, with the 'head' or the 'eye' broken off. It is of polished bone and was found in the Tŷ-isaf Neolothic chambered long cairn in Brecknockshire, and dates from c 2500 BC.

Two bone needles dating from the Early Bronze Age, c 1800–1400 BC are illustrated on page 56, the one on the left being a comparatively sophisticated type with a 'ring' head. Needles of this type are also known in bronze from the same era, and both are obviously an improvement on the simpler, ancestral forms. Also illustrated is an early bone weaving comb, found in the Lesser Garth Cave, at Radyr in Glamorganshire. This is very slender, about 7in long, and has a fine pointed end which may possibly have been used as an early form of stiletto, for making holes for a needle to pass through. With it was found an early awl, made of bone, which would have been used to pierce holes through hides, and then the thread, probably either strong sinews or strips of leather, would have been threaded through the holes.

D   55

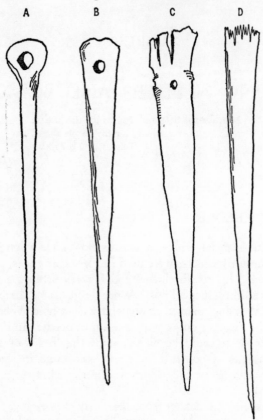

7 *Early Bronze Age needles, awl and weaving comb*
A—*Early Bronze Age bone needle, about 3in long, c 1600 BC*
B—*Bone needle, c 1800–1600 BC*
C—*Bone awl, c 1000 BC*
D—*Bone weaving comb, c 1000 BC*
   (All in National Museum of Wales, Cardiff)

The beautifully fashioned and highly polished needle dating from 1000 BC (page 43) was clearly the work of a true craftsman, even at that early period, and also comes from the Lesser Garth Cave. Illustrated on the same page is a bronze needle from Merthyr Mawr Warren, in Glamorganshire, of an even more advanced type, though of considerably later date. In this instance, two pieces of metal have been pressed together with a central loop left open, probably by a circular bone or other object having been slotted through it during the firing. This dates from about 300 BC and belongs to the 'La Tène' culture of the Iron Age, which has left so many traces, particularly in the lake villages around Glastonbury.

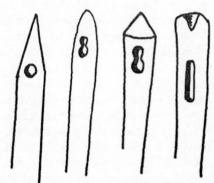

8   *Examples of typical ivory and bone Roman needles*
(In Caerleon Legionary Museum)

By Roman times, needles had achieved a variety of forms and the idea of a bodkin was beginning to emerge. The bone needles illustrated on this page come from the Caerleon Legionary Museum and are representative of the types of Roman needle frequently found in Britain. Although both bone and metal were being used for needles, the bone needle had the advantage in that it did not mark materials or rust. So far as steel needles are concerned, in England at least the climate was not conducive to the preservation of such metals as steel and, even if they were used here at any early period, none have remained. Bronze ones however did survive, as we have seen, and there are a number in museums still. Clearly most of them were never intended for fine sewing, but for use with the heavier materials such as leather, or the coarse canvases and sackings used in sails, tents and for packing goods. The finer types often have two or three eyes, which served to prevent the thread from slipping. In Medieval times a kink was sometimes made in the shaft of the needle to prevent it slipping in or out of the material if left for any length of time.

Roman writers mention needles made in gold and other precious metals and, unbelievably, set with gems. It would appear that right up to the Middle Ages the finest needles came from the East. The making of steel needles had been known in China for many centuries BC, and reached the Middle and Near East during the era of the Egyptian dynasties. We know from the craft remains of the ancient civilisations that they would have been capable of making steel needles as fine as any machine-made during our own day. Damascus, long famed for its skill in metalwork and steel, became a centre for fine needlemaking during the time of the Roman Empire, together with Antioch and other cities in the Near East. Fourteenth-century French inventories refer to '*aguilles d'Antioche*' (needles from Antioch) in terms which indicate that these items were highly prized and of great renown.

In the Middle Ages, needlemaking was one of the industries in which English monasteries engaged, but it is doubtful whether they ever made steel needles, or even knew of them. The usual method employed by needlers right up to Tudor times was a simple one, almost primitive, but completely effective for the coarser type of needle which was in general use. A piece of bronze wire of the requisite length was placed on an anvil and the eye end was flattened by a deft blow from a hammer: the eye was then punched out and cleared with a small, sharper punch. The point of the needle was filed down, and the head trimmed and smoothed. To complete the work, a guttering iron was used, and a groove was filed down both sides of the eye. Monasteries often employed lay-people and thus were the focus of a considerable amount of industry in their area, so that when they were dissolved by Henry VIII considerable hardship often resulted in the locality where their various industries were suddenly closed down. It is interesting to note that there is still a derelict needle mill on the site of Bordesley Abbey, near the great needlemaking centre of Redditch in Worcestershire.

By the sixteenth century, Antioch, Alexandria and Damascus were beginning to find themselves faced with competition for the European market from various centres, mainly in Italy and Spain which, by the end of the century, appear to have completely monopolised the industry. The Moorish invasions were not all loss to Spain, for the Moors brought with them many of their traditional skills and crafts, amongst them the secret of their fine steel and metal work, including the ability to make fine needles such as the West had not, up to that time, been able to produce.

So far as England is concerned, the manufacture of steel needles seems to have been introduced about 1543, though it was only towards the second part of the eighteenth century that it became established in France. For the most part, the finest needles in sixteenth-century England still came from Spain, and it is interesting to find that John Stowe, the antiquary, makes especial mention of needles in his famous *Survey of London and Westminster* of 1598. To him, as to most people of the day, a steel sewing needle was still a 'Spanish needle', since Cordoba was recognised as the most famous needlemaking centre in the West. He tells us: 'In Mary's time there was a Negro made fine needles in Cheapside, but would never teach his art to any,' and the man he refers to as a Negro was without doubt a Spanish Moor carrying on his own traditional and secret trades. Later in his book Stowe says that 'the art of making Spanish needles was first taught in England by Elias Crowse (or Krause), a German, about the eighth year of Queen Elizabeth'.

As the industry developed, the needlemakers in England formed themselves into a guild, the Worshipful Company of Needlemakers, and established themselves in Threeneedle Street, so called from the three needles depicted on their coat of arms, and later corrupted into Threadneedle Street. Unfortunately, the company came to resent the presence of any other, alien needlemakers, and as early as the beginning of the seventeenth century we find a petition filed forbidding the use of 'engines'. This had the effect of making many needlemakers move out of London to other localities. Eventually, in the eighteenth century, Redditch became a popular centre, largely because of its easy access to the water power necessary to the trade. A number of steel needlemakers were already established there, probably a remnant of the old monastic industry, and by the end of the century some 400 people were employed in the manufacture of needles and it was established eventually as the centre—the world centre as it has since turned out to be—of the needle industry.

We tend to associate needle manufacture with that of pins, presuming that the processes are similar, but in fact they vary considerably. Although, in time, the old medieval form of needlemaking was superseded by newer methods and by automatic machinery, even today the manufacture of needles is a finer operation and calls for greater skill than pinmaking.

In the first place, a superior quality of cast-steel wire is necessary. This is delivered in coils which have to be cut into short lengths, each length being sufficient to make two needles. Since the short lengths of wire are not perfectly straight it is necessary to rectify this fault before anything else can be done. The wires are therefore taken in bundles and an iron ring fitted over each end of the bundle. They are then placed in a stove and heated well, after which they are placed on an iron table, where a workman rolls them, still in the bundle, backwards and forwards, all the while pressing a curved bar, or 'rubbing knife', upon the body of the wires between the two rings. This operation, which calls for a high degree of skill, leaves the wires quite straight and regular by the rubbing of one wire against another under pressure.

The next process is the pointing of the needles which is effected by an automatic machine which presses the two ends of the wires against a revolving grindstone and thus forms the points. After this the needles, still in their twin-lengths, are taken to the stamping machine, where they are placed on the lower die. The upper die descends with such force that it forms the heads, makes the grooves below the needle-eye which assist in the threading of the needle, and almost pierces the eye itself. The 'eyeing' machine stamps the eye right through, but in so doing tends to leave the head of the needle slightly rough, so they have to be smoothed, or filed down, after which the wires are placed in a hand vice and cut through the middle, just above the two eyes. After this they have to be hardened and tempered, and then follows the process of scouring and burnishing. When this is complete, a drill has to be passed through the eye of each needle to make sure there is no roughness, and then the finishing room does its part. There, the needles are buffed with a special polishing composition, and the points ground again a little, since they tend to become slightly blunted during the cycle of the various operations. Any stains are removed, a final polishing is given, and then they are packeted up in the form in which they usually reach the purchaser.

Today we think of needles as being mainly used for doing embroidery, sewing and crewel work. But the list given by an old French needler of the trades of those who had used his services is enlightening. He enumerates: tailors, surgeons, gunners, hosiers, milliners, stocking makers, watchmakers, wax chandlers, drapers, scabbard makers, barbers, hairdressers, wig makers, etui makers (which includes those who made all manner of small containers from scissor cases to gun holsters), tobacconists and other similar workers, saddlers, silk workers, embroideresses, tapestry workers, candle makers, packers, oculists, engravers, goldsmiths, each needing special types of needle. The list also mentions compass needles, needles for knitting and for stringing pearls and other gems, for book binding, printers' press needles, and others. Faced with such a variety of form and purpose we realise that the needler's task in the old days must have been far more comprehensive than his counterpart's today, when many of the crafts mentioned have gone over to machine production and no longer require needles for hand sewing. The simple needles with which we seek to refurbish our carefully collected needlework boxes are a very small part of the whole story of the needle.

BODKINS

It would be difficult to state with any degree of certainty just when and where the dividing line arose between needles and bodkins. In Roman times and earlier the same article was in all probability used for both purposes. Right up until the end of the eighteenth century the terms were used indiscriminately, and the only distinguishing feature is the bodkin's slightly blunter end and larger eye, whilst the term was also often used for the hair ornaments described in Chapter 2, page 50. Small daggers or stilettos were also often referred to as bodkins, and the French terms for bodkin are interesting, being, on the one hand, *poinçon*, which can be used of a punch, a stiletto, or a small dagger, or *passe-lacet*, which relates it more nearly to its use as we understand it today.

It is in the sense of a dagger that Shakespeare uses the word bodkin in *Hamlet*:

> For who would bear the whips and scorns of time . . .
> When he himself might his quietus make
> With a bare bodkin?

By the sixteenth and seventeenth centuries, a bodkin was a very necessary item of toilet for both men and women; and the number of drawstrings, ribbons, cords and laces which needed fastening or threading and rethreading meant that it was often carried about on the person in a small needle or bodkin case to be on hand for emergency repairs. At this period bodkins were often quite large, up to 6 or 7in long at times, and were made in gold and silver, as well as commoner metals. They were frequently chased and engraved with a design incorporating the owner's initials, and often terminated in an ear-spoon or a snuff-spoon.

By the end of the eighteenth century, bodkins were becoming smaller again, and were frequently given as gifts. Many may still be found bearing the simple message 'Forget me not', or 'Ever love the giver', or else having commemorative dates engraved on them. They were frequently exchanged as betrothal gifts and the death of Princess Charlotte, in 1817, was the occasion for many bodkins to make their appearance engraved with her name and date of birth. Bodkins abounded during Queen Victoria's reign and commemorated the accession, wedding, jubilee, and other great events of her era. They are to be found made in ivory and bone as well as in silver and other metals.

CHAPTER 4

PINCUSHIONS AND NEEDLECASES

PINCUSHIONS

Since we know that pins have been costly for a considerable period of their history, we may reasonably expect to find receptacles for their safe keeping. The pincushion in its roughest form came into being very early in man's history, in the shape of a piece of flannel into which pins were stuck, or, alternatively, they were stuck into the material of the dress itself and kept on the person, thus forming a sort of permanent, living, pincushion. An interesting article in the *Queen*, dated 7 March 1903, says:

> . . . in those early days when pins of metal were costly and much-prized possessions, they were doubtless kept in some less insecure receptacle than an uncovered pincushion, and therefore the pin-box is probably a far less recent invention than the pincushion.

Silver pin-cases, or boxes, are known to have existed in the second part of the fourteenth century, but it is probable that pins were often kept with needles in the simplest forms of needlecases known to us, which are described later in the chapter. In the household accounts of Katharine, Countess of Devon, there is a record of the purchase, in 1524, of 'a pin case' costing the then quite expensive sum of sixteen pence, under the heading of 'necessaries for my lady', together with an item reading: '. . . 1000 white pins, 8d . . . ditto black, 7d.'

There is little to indicate just when pincushions, or pin-pillows, actually came into existence. In Tudor times an elaborate pincushion was certainly regarded as an acceptable gift to a lady of any status, and would seem to have been something of a novelty. When we read that in 1347, 12,000 pins were delivered from the royal wardrobe for the use of Princess Joan of France, or that Mary Tudor, as a girl, was provided with 10,000 pins as was considered to be fitting to her rank, we realise that they must have needed some sort of receptacle for their preservation. Probably the first pincushion came about as an expedient way of keeping a few pins at hand on the dressing-table without the necessity of opening a box each time. Amongst the New Year gifts received by Queen Elizabeth in 1562 was a fine, elaborately embroidered 'pyn-pyllow', and such an item was a highly prized possession. For the most part these 'pyn-pyllowes' were large, pillow-shaped, richly embroidered, and embellished with tassels, gold, coloured cords and silver lace. They might not be quite our taste in the twentieth century, but in those days they were in exact keeping with contemporary furnishings and dress and, when new, must have been very colourful and of a sumptuous appearance. In looking at old silks and fabrics it is always necessary to recall that two or three hundred years or more is a long time for colours to last, and so what may seem faded and dusty and dull to us now may originally have been brilliant enough. There is an interesting example of one of these Tudor 'pyn-pyllowes' in the Victoria & Albert Museum, in which the embroidery, on linen, consists of flowers, leaves, and fruit worked in silver and gilt threads and brightly coloured silks.

By the end of the seventeenth century, pincushions were becoming quite commonplace, but for the most part they still consisted of cushion or pillow shapes made in linen, canvas or satin, and embroidered with a variety of patterns according to the style of the times. Diamond and chevron-shaped designs from the late seventeenth century, and the scrolling fruit and flower designs of Jacobean days, can still be found in museums and private collections. There is a fine example of one of the latter in the Victoria & Albert Museum, covered with canvas and embroidered with coloured silks in a variety of stitches, with silver thread in short and chain stitching. Both the top and the reverse are covered with panels each bearing different devices—a lady with the ruff and full dress of the period, lions, unicorns, roses, fleurs-de-lis, animals and love knots, and the crowned letters I.R. (Iacobus Rex) standing for King James. Both at this time and also during the next century they were frequently made up from the rich brocades and costly gold and silver materials of discarded garments, and these have usually held their colour and lustre to a surprising extent.

From about the time of William and Mary onwards, the pillow shape began to be replaced by a circular form, sometimes set in a silver, or highly carved wooden, mount, and frequently on small feet. Some were also worn suspended from the waist by a long cord, as in the diagram seen below. About the same time small 'pyn-pyllowes' also came into vogue, with a silk cord attached, thus enabling them to be pinned into a pocket or a vanity bag. Small cylindrical cases known as pin-poppets, or pin-dollies, came into fashion too. These were normally made of wood, ivory or similar materials. Though not exactly boxes, they had lids which either screwed on or were sometimes hinged, and

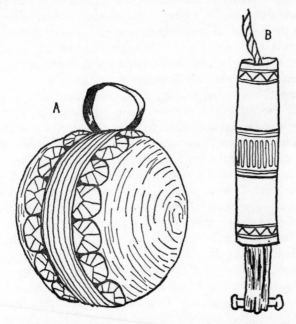

9 *Round pincushion of William and Mary period and early bone needlecase*
   A—Round pincushion of William and Mary period, worn suspended
     from waist. It is covered with green silk and silver thread and
     contained in a circular silver mount
   B—Early bone needlecase

were thus both safe and convenient. Some of the late eighteenth-century ones have a tiny stuffed pad of velvet fitted into the base so that pins could be fixed in securely. An example of such a pin-poppet may be seen in the photograph on page 71.

Pin-poppets were probably a development of the long, cylindrical form of needlecase, and the pin-case, such as is mentioned in the accounts of the Countess of Devon, and initially they were usually used for both pins and needles. About the mid-eighteenth century, however, they became specifically made to contain pins and, from being several inches in length became only about 2in high. In days when it was still customary for women to carry a small supply of pins about with them in order to be able to rectify any small mishap which might occur to their gowns or their many ruffles and laces, these pin-poppets were very popular and made charming little gifts, but they seem to have passed from fashion by the end of the eighteenth century, since few examples are known from the 1800s. Probably the rise of the Empire fashion, with its lack of pockets and its skimpier styles, had a good deal to do with their demise.

During Queen Anne's reign a popular occupation known as 'sticking pincushions' came into being. This had nothing to do with glue, gum, or any other form of adhesive, being simply a fashion for decorating pincushions with pins. These were inserted in such a way that the heads formed a pattern or spelt out a message, motto, or patriotic slogan such as 'God Bless the King and Queen', 'Ever True to You', 'Ever Love the Giver' and similar sentiments. The earliest known example of a pin-decorated pincushion is in the Victoria & Albert Museum, and bears the year 1652. Originally pink satin, it is now much faded, but the use of round-headed pins of different sizes to form the design of a vase of flowers, with a snail and a butterfly beside them, and the initials A.E. is both effective and pleasing. In general, such pincushions seem to have been at the height of their popularity from about 1750–1840.

'Manikins', or dummy pins, were sometimes used in these cushions instead of true pins, since to take out one pin in a moment of emergency might entirely ruin the message and the whole design. Marriage, death, birth, and all manner of other occasions, provided opportunities to convey the appropriate message in pin-sticking designs. We find white satin and lace cushions with 'God Bless the Bride' or 'May You be Happy' sent for weddings, and 'Long Live the Dear Child' or 'Welcome to the Babe' in pale pastel shades and spotted muslins for a new arrival. Mourning pincushions were suitably trimmed with black and had their condolences marked out in black mourning pins. One maternity pincushion linked with Byron's 'Mary'—Mary Chaworth—has a rose and a lily pricked on white satin with little forget-me-not sprays beside them, and the wording pricked in pins above and below: 'Hail to this teeming stage of strife; Hail, lovely miniature of life. Byron.'

'Welcome, little stranger' was a very common phrase for these maternity cushions, and America is particularly rich in such poetic phrases sometimes coupled with contemporary allusions. One, given to a Boston baby born during the siege says, 'Welcome, little stranger, Though the port is closed.' An early nineteenth-century one says 'God assist the mother through her danger, And protect the little stranger', and another 'Peace, prosperity, and joy, Attend the little girl or boy'.

During the eighteenth century, pins became cheaper and easier to buy from the itinerant pedlar or the market stall, so pincushions increased in popularity, and every needlewoman in the country seems to have tried her skill at making new shapes and styles out of every possible sort of material. Many began to combine pin-sticking with embroidery, and in late Georgian times little circular pincushions became popular again which combined the fashion for pin-sticking with embroidered texts or messages. These pocket pin-pads vary from just over an inch across, to nearly 3in. Usually they are made from two circles of card laid close together and covered with material and embroidered with silks and the tiny ribbons of the period or, at a later date, with beadwork. The pins were inserted round the edge, and gradually the padding between the two sides increased in size and became about half an inch or so in depth, which of course increased the number of pins which could be inserted, but tended to lose the effect of pin-sticking. Sometimes they were made up of a length of coloured ribbon terminating in a small cushion which then had its embroidered covers sewn on to it sandwich-fashion. Gradually they were made with bone, ivory, mother-of-pearl, and wood covers, and many of these are inlaid or carved, as with the examples on page 71. There is a strong French influence about many of them, and it is believed that they, together with the straw-work boxes and articles found in this era, are often the work of the French prisoners of war from Napoleonic times.

Pin-balls, usually knitted and stuffed with cotton wool, were in great vogue from about 1720 onwards. This is a style which lasted longer than almost any other type of pincushion and can be found right up to the middle of the nineteenth century. Throughout all this time, pin-balls were remarkably consistent, not only in shape but in the actual patterns used in the knitting. They were worn swinging from the waist on a cord, and very often bear the initials of their owner, as well as the date, and sometimes a patriotic or religious phrase. A pin-ball in Gloucester Folk Museum bears the legend 'M. Hooper 1800' and there are several in the Victoria & Albert Museum dating from the early 1700s up to the first half of the nineteenth century. The 1745 Rebellion has interesting connections with pincushions. One favourite pincushion inscription amongst Bonnie Prince Charlie's many supporters was 'God Bless P.C.', and sometimes, even more emphatically, 'God Bless P.C. and Down with the Rump'. Hibbert Ware's *History of the Foundation of Manchester* mentions the Whigs growing intolerant of the popularity of Prince Charlie, and thinking of setting up a 'Manufacture Committee to visit the warehouses from time to time, inspect the goods, and severely punish all such persons as shall be found to have any objects which emblematically favour Popery or the Pretender. . . . As for your pincushion makers, I think they should be rigorously chastised and their works publicly burned, let the pretty misses cry as they will. . . .' No English loom could safely have made these pincushions, and they are believed to have come over from France, via Scotland. The pin-balls were attached to a suspender which hung on to the girdle, much in the fashion of a chatelaine.

Sadder memories are conjured up by the very rare pincushions which bear the names of men who died for Prince Charles. Usually these are arranged in four circles round a central design which bears the shape of the conventional Tudor rose surrounded by the words 'Mart. for K. and cou' (Martyred for King and Country) and the date 1746. On one side are the names of generals and leaders—Kilmarnock, Derwentwater, Lovat, Balmerino, etc—as well as those of the men, and on the other are the names of esquires and captains. One such pincushion, in the Ashmolean Museum at Oxford, is in a very sad state of decay but has an interesting story attached to it. It was found during repairs to Bampton Deanery House, Oxfordshire, together with a deal box containing a hen's egg on which was written 'God bless King James III'. Inside the box was a paper with the following resolution:

> I put this in with a designe not to oppen itt till King James comes to the crowne, and I will cape my word itt is a hen's egge, and some of Martha Frederick's haire and her Mother's haire in this Box. I will for ever stick to my principles. I will ever honour my King as long as I live. Martha Frederick.

On the other side of the paper was written 'Do not open this peaper for fere of yr eyes, for it will blind you' and on the lid of the box 'It is a forfit to open this box, for it is congering in it and will eat out yr eyes'. It would seem that Martha Frederick did indeed 'cape her word' and, unhappily for her, the occasion never arose when she could open her box and rejoice in the accession of King James III.

In the Victoria & Albert Museum there is an interesting example of a different style of pincushion from the late eighteenth century which testifies to the fervour of the abolitionists of slavery. This is a circular pincushion bearing an inset medallion of a chained and kneeling slave. Above his head is the message 'LORD release the captive', and this was probably one of many on sale at the bazaars, or sales of work, then becoming popular.

From the dawn of the nineteenth century, pincushions burst forth into a tremendous diversity of form and excellence. Many are stitched with the finest imaginable stitchery, and the pins used are the smallest size available, namely the ribbon pins of just under half an inch in length. Others have texts worked in fine cross stitch, and were clearly intended more for decorative and 'religious' purposes than for use. About 1820, printed silk, disc, pocket pincushions began to be made, usually showing views of well-known buildings, country scenes, or bearing commemorative details of popular events or of deceased personages of note. In the latter case the pins round the cushion are once again the black mourning pins. These types of pincushions were very popular as wedding gifts, for the bride to carry in her reticule and in her other luggage. They bore some suitable message of goodwill: 'May you be happy' or 'May good fortune go with you'.

But the Victorian era was, perhaps, the heyday of the pin-cushion. They were made in every conceivable shape. Fruits were much in vogue, strawberries in particular, since their pitted surface lent itself to reproduction by the use of pinheads studded into red velvet or silk. Fans, shoes, tiny baskets of flowers and fruit, wheelbarrows, tiny coaches, little goblets and cups, jockey caps, books, bellows, hearts, dolls, even tiny animals, all were represented in a score of shapes and materials to rejoice the hearts of all who saw them and to demonstrate the skill and ingenuity of their makers. One charming specimen seen recently was made in the shape of a miniature cottage loaf, and is so realistic in colour and to the touch that it is often mistaken for the real thing.

Beadwork was of course popular, but there was less scope for it in pincushions, apart from the flat, two-sided, circular ones with pins inserted all round the circumference leaving a free space to be worked with beads on the top and bottom surfaces in the same way as in the needlecase on page 144. There are still a number of these about, but on the whole it was a type of work which lent itself more to other articles. One successful method of using beadwork combined with stitchery is in the Gloucester Folk Museum, where a rectangular pincushion has been worked in chequerboard design of red tapestry stitching and white bead squares, with a thick fringe surrounding it composed entirely of loops of beads. Another popular type of pincushion was leather or material combined with raffia-work (plate, page 144).

From about the middle of the Victorian era right up to the Edwardian age, we find pincushions beginning to increase not only in size but in complexity, until they were more in the nature of free-standing ornaments for the dressing-table than anything else, and frequently were obviously designed more as what we would

Page 71 (above) *Straw-work needlework box in the shape of a book, fitted inside with lidded compartments. A French paper covered casket, c 1800, with mother-of-pearl corners, feet and tools. Also two needleboxes and an ivory pin poppet; (below) Indian carved sandalwood workbox fitted inside with rectangular lidded compartments. Beside it, an early 19th-century mother-of-pearl thimble with gold rim, carved ivory needlecase, two circular pincushions and a mid Victorian black net and beadwork wallet-purse*

Page 72 (above) *American workbox 1791, in birdseye maple case, made for Mrs Benedict Arnold. The Indian style fitments are birchbark bound with green ribbon, the lids covered with white satin, delicately embroidered a l'Anglaise, with floral sprays;* (below) *Victorian velvet and brass scrollwork casket, containing reel-holders, ruler, penknife, bodkin, stiletto, needle, scissors, pencil, tambour hook, yard measure and needlecase and thimble. Beside it, the contrasting simplicity of a maplewood 'Shaker' box 1836*

now call 'gimmickry'. Many became ornate and clumsy in their too-lavish ornamentation, and by the early part of the present century their day was nearly over. Today the pincushion is more often than not an object of sheer utility, having frequently degenerated into a plastic pin-box, with its long history of elegance and ingenuity for the most part completely forgotten. Nevertheless, in order to furnish a workbox aright, it is as well to have some idea of what could have been appropriately included at any given date, and then to collect carefully and with discrimination until the piece that exactly suits the particular box for which it is intended is found. With so wide a range in both dates and styles there is every likelihood that, in this field, a collector's zeal will be well rewarded.

NEEDLECASES

Turning to needlecases, these probably were known in a simple form even in classical times, but no absolutely certain examples have come down to us. There are, as mentioned earlier, certain objects from Anglo-Saxon graves in Great Britain which are sometimes identified as needlecases or needlework cases, but which may well be amulets. Since, on the Continent, they are found only in Christian graves, it is very probable that they were of Christian origin and used as reliquaries, being taken over as loot by the Saxon invaders and then used by their womenfolk, who are known to have been fine needlewomen, as containers for their sewing aids.

When we come to medieval times, however, we find a form of needlecase which, as with so many personal requisites, was worn suspended by a cord from the girdle. The most usual type was a short piece of bone or wood, hollowed out to enable it to move up and down when a cord was threaded through it. A piece of soft material was sewn on to the cord at the lower end, into which the needles were affixed, and then a ring or small bolt was attached to this to prevent the tube slipping right off (diagram, page 65). When the needles were not needed the tube of wood covered them, and when wanted it was pulled up leaving them exposed for use. It was simple but entirely effective. Some such needle-

E

cases were, of course, fashioned in more sophisticated forms and materials, a fish in silver or other metal being a favourite form since, in Christian countries, a fish was a symbol for our Lord, the letters of the Greek word *ichthus* (fish) standing for the first letters of each of the Greek words in the sentence 'Jesus Christ, Son of God, Saviour of the world'. Slightly later in the Middle Ages, others, of a flattened type and frequently lozenge shaped were made, since this meant that the surface could be decorated more liberally, or encrusted with gems and mosaics in more elaborate forms. Eventually this, in its turn, gave way to a rectangular shape, and with the advent of the steel needle during Tudor times, most needlecases took the form of needlebooks. For several centuries this continued to be the most usual method of keeping needles, but since any dampness in the climate meant that the 'pages' absorbed moisture from the atmosphere causing the needles to rust, it was not an ideal method of storage. Gradually, therefore, small cylindrical containers came into being about the beginning of the eighteenth century, the simplest being plain boxes. More elaborate styles can be found, in the shape of little standing figures of peasants, fisher-folk, or other workers, and about 3in high, but these are mainly of continental make and more frequently to be found on the mainland of Europe than in England or America.

Cylindrical needlecases from the eighteenth century onwards are still available to collectors in a wide variety of styles, shapes, and materials. For the most part, so far as form goes, they follow a fairly standard pattern, being about 3in long, or sometimes up to about 5in, with the top unscrewing from the bottom half. They are of silver, gold, carved ivory or tortoiseshell, enamel, bone, and various woods. The workmanship is often extremely fine and delicate, and these little cases greatly enhance the beauty and value of any needlework box.

Gradually needlecases received the same treatment as other sewing accessories, and began to be made in a variety of shapes, very often more as 'toys' than as articles for serious use. We need to remember that the word 'toy', in most centuries other than our own, referred to any small article, often fashioned of precious metals and extremely expensive, which might serve to delight the eye and excite wonderment in the viewer. It might have either a decorative or a useful purpose, but it was essentially 'a thing of joy', a curiosity, and the word did not indicate solely a plaything for children. As such, needlecases came under the general term of *bijouterie*, and were ingeniously shaped into umbrellas and parasols, daggers in scabbards, quivers of arrows, the tower of a castle, the spire of a church, or a dozen other curious forms. A very lovely example, in the shape of a pea-pod, and probably c 1800, may be seen on page 143. This is so beautifully fashioned in ivory that, although the interior holds only a plain rectangular fitting for the needles, when the fingers are run along the outside of the pod it feels as though there actually are peas inside. Some needlecases were just plain cylinders, gaining their beauty from their simple elegance of style and decoration. On these, as on so many other tools, may often be found the phrases common to the period such as '*Gage de mon amitie*', or its English equivalent 'A Token of my Esteem', and other graceful sentiments, or the delicate panels of tiny flower sprays so dear to both eighteenth- and nineteenth-century hearts. The china containers from Battersea, Bristol and other factories, with their lovely enamelled flower sprays are much sought after.

About the end of the eighteenth century, beaded cases were extremely popular. These fitted round an inner container, each row of minute beads on their fine wire threads being sewn to the next row by the smallest stitches imaginable. They can usually be distinguished from later examples of the Victorian craze for beadwork by the fact that their beads are much smaller and finer, and the stitching of the eighteenth and early nineteenth centuries is far neater and smaller. It is, indeed, incredible that anyone could achieve such minute and accurate stitchery. The stitches on shoes of, for instance, the Carolean period, are so tiny, so exquisitely even, both on the silken heels and the leather soles, that it is hardly conceivable that they were made by hand. It was this delicacy of stitchery which remained on through the eighteenth and early nineteenth centuries, and which can be seen also in the fine tent and cross stitch of the era. By contrast, the later Victorian stitching was, in general, far less noteworthy. These little beadwork cases are very charming, and a sought-for addition to any collection.

Flat, rectangular needlecases were also known during the same period, sometimes in wood, but more normally in mother-of-pearl or ivory, often with enamel or *verre églomise* panels and with sliding drawers for holding the needles. But these were usually of French or Italian origin and the style was only seldom followed in England, where they are often taken to be cardcases.

The cylindrical form continued to be popular during Victorian times, but tended to become more ornate and heavy in design as time went by. Needleboxes, as shown in plate, page 71, about 2in–3in high and looking rather like miniature knife boxes, became popular, with sloping lids which meant that packets of needles of different sizes and lengths could fit inside and be easily seen, the larger being at the back and the smaller towards the front. A little later, from about the middle of the century onwards, the needlebook came strongly back into favour once more. Ivory and mother-of-pearl covers, similar to those of a *carnet de bal*, are frequently found, together with polished wood covers sometimes inlaid or with marquetry and very often with prints of notable places on them (plate, page 144). But the most usual form gradually came to be the homemade type of needlework case which enabled the embroideress to show off her skill in a variety of forms. Sets of perforated cards could be purchased—rectangular, oval, or circular in shape—which were then decorated with a neat pattern of coloured silks worked through the punched holes, usually in cross stitch, and frequently embellished with high-minded sentiments and religious texts. It is particularly in these later types of needlecase that the difference may be clearly seen between the tiny, neat cross stitch of the previous century and the comparatively large version of the stitch in late Victorian times. Nevertheless, even when from a technical point of view the actual stitchery was of a lower standard than that of earlier years, a great deal of time and effort went into the work and most of these small articles denote hours of patient work and loving thought. The multi-coloured hexagonal beadwork needlebook (plate, page 144) dates from about 1850, and is a good example of such painstaking effort. 'Whatsoever thy hand findeth to do, do it with all thy might' could well have been the motto engraved upon the heart of even the youngest Victorian!

'Housewives' or 'hussifs' have also always been a popular form of needlecase, from medieval times onwards, but eighteenth- and nineteenth-century ones began to receive more ornamental treatment than their forebears. They are usually about 8–12in long when unfolded, with a needlebook and pincushion at one end, and carefully stitched channels up the main body of the hussif through which coloured silks could be slotted to keep them smooth and untangled. In the days when skeins of silk or twist were expensive and not always easily available, and when they had to be wound by hand on to spools before use, it was of the utmost importance that they should be kept safe and clean before they were needed, and the slots down the hussif were an eminently practical method of ensuring this.

The variety of hussifs made so patiently, carefully, and with such painstaking stitching is endless. A very lovely one, probably c 1790–1800, is at Dyrham Park near Bath, where each fold is decorated with tiny flowers and marked with the size of the needle to be found there. It is a simple, but dainty, reminder of days more leisured than our own. Many needlecases and hussifs are in the form of a book, either folding up to represent one, or else slotting into a small separately made container resembling a book, and often bearing the legend 'Essays' or 'A Stitch in Time' or 'To Right the Wrong'.

Things moved more swiftly in the nineteenth century than they had in earlier times, and needle manufacturers began to sell needles in small leather and gilt boxes and 'books', and in coloured cardboard boxes with pictures on the lid, usually of well-known places such as Windsor Castle and Buckingham Palace, or depicting stirring scenes from recent history. In the patriotic fashion of the day many such boxes bear pictures of Britannia and Proserpina, the Lion and the Unicorn, or the portraits of Queen Victoria and Prince Albert. Many of the earliest of these boxes bore designs by Baxter on their lids; these prints came later to be known as needle-prints and were much sought after. Any collector able to furnish a workbox with one of these tiny, beautifully made, gilt boxes may justifiably feel that something worthwhile has been achieved.

Advertising had started up in earnest during Queen Victoria's long reign, and many firms used etuis, needlecases and other small articles to convey their name and message to the public, such as 'Use Hudson's Soap' or other appropriate invitations and reminders.

Interesting examples of late Victorian days are the metal gilt needlecases in the form of a folding screen, each leaf being carefully numbered with needle sizes. Sometimes small, flat, circular metal boxes may also be found which have a number of holes round the circumference, each bearing a different number, this being the size of the needle contained in that particular segment of the box. When the flat disc surrounding the box is moved round to leave a particular hole uncovered, the needles may be shaken out of the hole, one at a time, ready for use. The disc is then moved on slightly and all the needles are kept safe again within their metal prison.

Handmade needlecases still abounded in very diverse forms, but they were beginning to become too large and too ornate to qualify as things of any beauty. One needlecase seen recently was made in the shape of a leaf, decorated with white beads and with dried fish scales sewn on to it to form a pattern. Ingenious, perhaps, but with a slight touch of the macabre about it! Another, in the shape of a guitar, was some 10in long and made out of red velvet and decorated with beadwork and tassels. Yet another, about the same size, was in the form of a banner complete with heraldic device, cords, tassels, and upright and cross poles. Some were in the form of dolls, the various skirts lifting to reveal the flannel petticoats set with needles and sometimes holding a basket full of pins.

But the needlecase had almost come to the end of its era of playfulness and elegance. The last days of the Victorian, and the beginning of the Edwardian eras, saw a decline in both beauty of workmanship and originality of design. Sober leather needlepouches and wallets, convenient and practical, are found in abundance, and also cases which are souvenirs and momentoes; but needlework itself was fast going out of fashion as an indispensable accomplishment for young ladies of refinement, and needlecases, together with needle-boxes, were becoming more and more prosaic and utilitarian.

CHAPTER 5

THIMBLES AND THIMBLE CASES

THIMBLES

One of the tales with which children are familiar from earliest days is that of Thumbelina, the little maiden who was so very small that she could fit into a thimble, or thumbel, and whose dainty bed was made from a walnut shell most delicately carved and polished. Illustrations of Thumbelina's thimble usually depict this small article with great delicacy, and often it is of china and ornamented with delicate sprays of flowers. It is unfortunate that the plastic variety of thimble of our own day should be so lacking in imagination, since, working under far more difficult circumstances, all other centuries have done their best to pour creative skill into even so small an article as this, to the endless delight of children looking through their mothers' needlework boxes in later years.

The German word for a thimble is *fingerhut*, which, translated literally, means 'finger-cap', or 'finger-hat', and is delightfully descriptive. The French word is *dé*, and the Spanish *dedal*, both derived from the Latin *digitus*, meaning a 'finger'. The English word comes from Anglo-Saxon *thymel* (related to German *daumen* meaning 'thumb') which became corrupted into 'thimmel', 'thimbil', or sometimes 'thumbel'. In the poem mentioned in the first chapter of this book Thomas Occleve, c 1370, uses the term 'themel'. These thumbels, themels, thimbils, or thimmels, consisted of a piece of strong leather stitched up one side, with a leather cap sewn in across the top, much in the manner of a finger-stall used on a bandaged finger. Examples may still be found in some parts of England and in the South of Ireland, and also in

Canada and some Eastern countries. Roman metal thimbles of the type to which we today are accustomed, were well known in England in earlier centuries, and it is only after the Dark Ages that the term 'themel' in its varied spellings, became used.

Thimbles have, for a very long time, had more than utilitarian value. For several centuries it was the custom to reward the small, diligent embroideress with a silver thimble 'cunningly engraved and writ upon' when her sampler had attained a degree of perfection which merited praise, and of course, this treasured gift was also an inducement to further efforts. In the heyday of the great courts of Europe, from the time of the Medici to the last tragic days of the Czarist régime, Court jewellers turned their attention and efforts to every article which could in any way be embellished and beautified for my lady's pleasure and use. Thimbles and thimble cases were no exception.

Thimbles themselves range from bronze and iron, through steel, silver, gold, to china and even glass. Many have charming mottoes inscribed upon them, or small verses of poetry, or Biblical texts. A whole world of gracious living is expressed in the phrases found upon some of these dainty gifts: 'A token of my affection', 'A token of my esteem', 'Forget me not', '*Gage de mon amitié*', '*Bin ich deine*' ('I Am Yours'). For whilst it would not have been permissible to receive an expensive piece of jewellery from a gentleman, a lady could with propriety accept such a harmless token of esteem as a thimble or thimble case. And what joy it must have been to the donor to know that his small gift would frequently adorn that dainty finger, and that he himself would be remembered as she stitched industriously away at her work.

It was during the mid-nineteenth century that a completely erroneous idea became current in England that thimbles had been invented at the end of the seventeenth century, and no earlier. In Haydn's *Dictionary of Dates* which appeared in 1855, and which was a great educational standby in Victorian drawing-rooms, the following paragraph is to be found:

THIMBLES. This . . . is of Dutch invention. The art of making them was brought to England by John Lofting, a mechanic from Holland, who set up a workshop at Islington, near London, and practised the manufacture of them in various metals, with profit and success, about 1695.

Since thimbles of a considerably earlier date than this have been found, and since they are mentioned in numerous places in literature and old inventories, it is clear that the author was either mistaken in his belief, or else that he intended to state that the said John Lofting had invented a new *method* of thimble making. This was indeed likely, since the Dutch were clever mechanics, and it is very probable that they had invented a new device for the manufacture of thimbles which was an improvement on old methods, and which accorded Lofting the 'profit and success' with which, it is gratifying to learn, his labours were apparently blessed.

By 1876, when the *Dictionary of Dates* was revised by Benjamin Vincent, this error had obviously been brought to the notice of the publishers, since this edition states:

THIMBLES are said to have been found at Herculaneum. The art of making them was brought to England by John Lofting . . .

Unfortunately, by that time the notion was firmly established that thimbles were a comparatively recent innovation, so no efforts were made to inquire into their early stages of development.

It is believed that the art which John Lofting did introduce into England was that of sand-casting, which had only recently been discovered on the Continent. Since there was a supply of suitable sand in the area, he opened a workshop at Islington, and began to manufacture cast thimbles in large numbers. It is debatable, however, whether in fact the new method was really superior to the older process, since when the thimbles were removed from the casting mould they were in a very rough state and required a considerable amount of work before they were in any way comparable to the older type of thimble.

Earliest Thimbles

So far as we can know, the earliest form of thimble was probably a sort of shield, made simply of bone, or wood, bound on to the finger. Thimbles made from bone are amongst the simplest and most primitive types known. Square pieces of stone, grooved and indented, have been found in Egypt, and these are claimed to be a very early form of 'needle-pusher' (diagram, page 82). We know almost nothing of early British thimbles. As mentioned previously, our word 'thimble' derives from the Anglo-Saxon *thymel*, which denoted an entirely different type of finger covering, as will be seen later; but two words in the older British tongue indicate that early thimbles were made either of bronze or iron, or of some other material selected for protection rather than adornment. The word *gwyniadur* or *gwniadur*, still used today as the Welsh word for thimble, means, literally, a 'sewing-steel'; the other word *byswain* means 'finger-guard' or 'shield'. Both words seem to imply that the ancient Britons looked for almost a form of armour as they fashioned their skin garments or sewed together the tough hides which formed their bed coverings and door cur-

10 *An early Egyptian stone needle-pusher, approx 1¾in high.*
Believed to be c 2000 BC

tains. By classical times, however, Britain was famous for the beautiful woollen, multi-coloured plaid-like garments which her people wore, which were skilfully and beautifully fashioned and greatly admired by both Greeks and Romans. The picture of skin-clad savages is unrealistic, and bears about as much relation to truth as it would be to say of our modern habit of wearing fur coats against the winter cold that it indicates that the wearers are savages!

As far as may be ascertained from the specimens remaining to us, the early thimbles of the classical era were of the two varieties which still exist in similar forms in the Western world today. The first is normally referred to as the 'ring' type. This was formed by a strip of metal simply rolled round to form a band,

or ring, usually about ¾in wide and soldered at the join. This left
the ends open, and the thimble was slipped over the top joint of
the finger, leaving the tip unprotected. In certain types of sewing
—more particularly in sewing very heavy materials—it is the side
of the finger, and not the top, which is used for pushing the
needle through the fabric, so in these types of work a covered end
would be superfluous and even cumbersome.

The other variety with which we in the West are most familiar
is known as the 'sugar-loaf'. In this, the tip of the finger has been
protected by having a covered top. In Greek and Roman examples
the tops are often of a very defined conic shape, and the whole
thimble is only about 1in high. In later centuries, in Spain and
elsewhere, this conical type appeared again in a larger and longer
form, sometimes being nearly 2¾in high, and two examples of this
sugar-loaf, slightly pointed type, are given in the diagram below.
These conical types have not been used in Europe for the last
four or five centuries, the domed type having eventually gained in
public favour.

11 *Three bronze cast thimbles from Spain. The second and third come from
Granada and Cordova respectively 12–13th century, and are approx 2in high
(In Victoria & Albert Museum, London)*

The pointed sugar-loaf type seems to have been made in one
piece, being punched or moulded according to the metal used,
whereas the later domed, or rounded types, more popular during
the Middle Ages, was usually made in two sections. In both, the
apexes were frequently left quite smooth, especially in the longer
or taller types, only the main body being pounced, except for the

plain band around the rim which seems to have been a feature of most thimbles. Pounce marks taken all the way down to the bottom would probably result in the needle slipping and injuring the finger, whereas a plain band at the bottom means that the wearer is forced to use only the upper section. In nearly all ages and countries, the plain finishing band is found on both ring and sugar-loaf types. Whether or not pounce marks continued all the way up and over the apex of the sugar-loaf thimble seems to have been very much left to the whim of the individual doing the pouncing, but in fact, the more sharply defined the point, the less need there was for pouncing, since obviously the top could not be used for pushing the needle through and only the side must have been used. On the squatter, more rounded types, pounce marks could have been useful and there was more chance that the top would be used in sewing. Towards the beginning of this present century a bronze thimble (diagram, below) was found in England at Verulamium (St Albans) by a famous archaeologist, which, after careful examination and comparison, has been accepted as Roman.

12 *Roman 'ring type' thimble found in ruins of Herculaneum;*
and Roman bronze thimble found at Verulamium

If we compare this with the medieval thimble discovered at Weoley Castle, near Birmingham (diagram, page 85) it will be seen that the latter has, to our eyes, a more modern form with its rounded top and more slender body. The nearest dating which can be given for this AD 1400–1550.

With the fall of the Roman Empire, Europe was plunged into disorder for several centuries, and it is only in fairly recent years that it has been possible for us to form any definite picture of what life must have been like during those years, usually known as the Dark Ages. Perhaps the archaeologists at present working on the finds at Cadbury Hill in Somerset and elsewhere will excavate a hidden hoard of thimbles, but otherwise there is at present very little indeed to denote how the English ladies or the artisans of those times did their sewing, or what tools they used. So far as the Continent is concerned, we know that there were bone thimbles made during and probably after the time of the Roman occupation. But so far as the writer has been able to trace there are none of these early bone types extant in England today. Medieval thimbles, however, abound, ranging from about AD 1200 up to the end of the fifteenth century. For the most part, however, the thimbles which remain to us today would appear to date from about AD 1400 onwards. It is these medieval types which indicate most clearly the difference between the 'sugar-loaf' type of earlier days and the 'domed', or rounded, top.

13 *Medieval thimble of type found at Weoley Castle; two other medieval thimbles, probably of somewhat later date, found during excavations in London Wall*

The Themel

In England at any rate, from the beginning of the Dark Ages until the twelfth or thirteenth centuries, the metal thimble seems to have been very largely replaced by the leather 'themel' referred to at the beginning of the chapter. Different forms of needlework demand different methods of work, and different races use the same tools differently or, alternately, use completely different ones. The Scandinavian people have always been noted for their embroidery and needlecraft, and in their invasions of the British Isles they brought with them not only their native skills but, apparently, also the tools they used. They did not use a thimble of the Roman type, but the thummel, by which we deduce that they tended to *pull* the needle through, rather than push it, which would entail something in the nature of the ring or sugar-loaf types. But from being worn originally on the thumb, which would be practical for working on flat, fairly soft surfaces held in the hand, it gradually became used on the finger instead, very probably during the time of the famous *opus Anglicanum*, or goldwork period c 1250–1350, and the name lingered on with its reminder of its original usage. It is interesting to note, in this connection, that the Continental names for thimble tend to retain their Roman origin, and clearly had no Scandinavian influences, whereas England, time and again invaded by 'the men from the north', took on the language of her invaders and their type of tool, even though ultimately reverting to the metal type of finger protection.

Certainly as early as AD 900 Englishwomen were noted for the excellence of their embroidery, and no art comes into existence within a generation alone; it takes time for it to be formulated, to grow, and finally to flower in its full glory. There are records dating back to the end of the seventh century mentioning the skill of the English embroideresses, and it was at this period that St Etheldreda made 'with her own hands' the famous stole and maniple for St Cuthbert, richly ornamented with gold and precious stones, which is today one of the treasures of Durham Cathedral.

It certainly seems that however barbaric the times had been, or still were, the Anglo-Saxon women cultivated a natural talent which seems to have been particularly expended upon the ecclesiastical vestments and furnishings of the day. Yet, at the very time when one would have expected metal thimbles to abound, so that they would turn up under every stone today, archaeologists have found little or no trace of any such article. Anyone who has done any quantity of gold work will perhaps be able to see the reason for this surprising lack. In this type of work, a metal thimble is of little use, especially when working at a frame on the heavy backing needed for a large frontal, a heavy banner, or other large pieces. Indeed, it is a hindrance, since it can often slip and be cumbersome, and no matter how dedicated the worker, cut and bleeding fingers must be attended to and will certainly impair craftsmanship. It is probable that bandaged fingers first suggested the sensible protection of a leather 'thummel', which leaves the finger supple and sensitive, yet protected against the steel of the needle-blade. For it is not the tip of the finger so much as the side which is used in this work, for pulling through the needle against the stiff backing on the unyielding tautness of the frame, and a plain leather finger-stole is the answer to all the problems.

Medieval to 1700

With the passing of the great era of the *opus Anglicanum*, or 'the English work', with the disaster of the Black Death, the ordinary metal thimble gradually seems to have come back into its own again. On the Continent it would appear that the themel type had never quite taken over—perhaps because there was comparatively little goldwork done there, England being the world centre for the art, and perhaps because there had been less Scandinavian influence. In a very notable work, *Les Accessoires du Coutume et du Mobilier*, by H. R. D'Allemagne, there are some well-documented details and instances connected with the study of the history of thimbles in France. In the thirteenth century there were two corporations there engaged in the manufacture of these articles: those of latten or of brass were made by the *fermailleurs*, or clasp and buckle makers, whilst the button-makers, or *boutonniers*, fashioned theirs of iron or copper. Those making thimbles as well as clasps or buttons, were known as *déeliers*, or *déiliers*.

During the fourteenth century, French thimbles began to be more lavishly decorated, far earlier, it would seem, than their counterparts across the Channel. Often their owners' crests or coats-of-arms were inscribed on them; then sprays of foliage and ornamental motifs in relief work made their appearance in place of the old, time-honoured prick marks, and a silver or gold band would frequently be embellished with an inscription or a motto. The continental thimble makers clearly had the lead over their English contemporaries, since our thimbles of the same era were very plain and simple, and the themmel was still in common use by the population at large.

As regards methods of manufacture, by the fifteenth century at least there are indications that a lathe was being used in the making of the indentations. Where this method was used, the thimble would be fitted to a chuck, and then revolved with a knurled wheel pressed against it, forming the markings in a fairly even pattern. From a cup in the form of a thimble, believed to be a replica of the ordinary thimble of the day, and made to the order of the Tailors' Guild of Nuremberg, Germany in 1586, we can see the various advances made in the methods of manufacture. Here, the indents are knurled in, but it would appear that several wheels have been mounted together. This method has been perfected and is now in common use, but it is evident that as early as the Nuremberg thimble-cup, inscriptions and parts of the decoration were rolled on by the same method, the pattern being cut intaglio on a narrow roller and then pressed into the thimble as it revolved on the chuck.

Some medieval brass thimbles were, as already mentioned, made in one piece, but at quite an early date and, certainly by the Middle Ages, thimbles were being made in two pieces. That is to say, the body of the thimble was made from a piece of sheet-metal rolled into a hollow tube, with a soldered seam. The cap was then made separately and fitted on to the body. There are a number of examples of early thimbles made in this fashion, notably in the British Museum and in the London Museum. The tin with which they were soldered has gradually perished over the years so that the joints have opened and it is possible to see the method of manufacture. From the examples in the London Museum, approximately fifteenth and sixteenth century in origin, it is evident that the later the date of manufacture, the more likelihood there is of their being made in two pieces. The reason for the change of method is not certain, but it is probably simpler to make a neat ring type and then add a flattish dome, so the practice became more or less generally adopted. It also resulted in a smaller and neater article being achieved in many cases. This cannot, however, be the full reason, since some very minute thimbles are known which are made in one piece, but, generally speaking, the thinner the metal became, the more likelihood there was of a thimble being made in two pieces.

There are several interesting mentions of thimbles in an article entitled 'On Thimbles' by H. Syer Cuming, in the *Journal of the British Archaeological Association* for 1879. One example mentioned

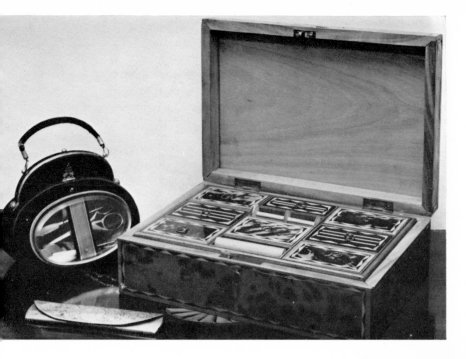

Page 89 (above) *Turtleshell workbox, c 1820, with tortoiseshell and painted cedarwood compartments inside; a small Victorian vanity bag in claret coloured velvet with bevelled glass front, fitted with tools. The late 19th-century silver crochet-hook case in the foreground is lined with purple velvet; (below) late 17th- or early 18th-century sewing box in polished wood case, with purple velvet lining and polished steel stiletto and seam-presser combined, scissors, thimble, and needlecase*

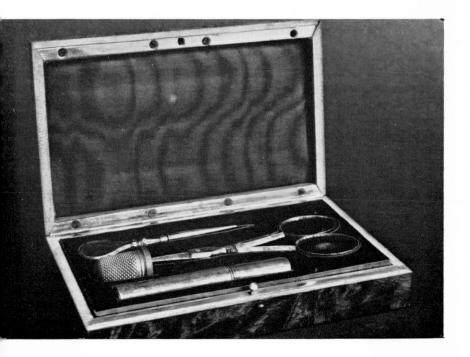

Page 90   (above) *Paper-covered casket, late 1800s. 'Jane's Box' and another smaller, wooden box, early 19th-century and a circular 6-reel container. Note holes for threads when in use;* (below) *early 19th-century French satinwood workbox, with painted scenes on lid and sides, and a formal inlay border round the lid. The interior is lined with deep carmine silk*

'has the lower band stamped with a little shield charged with a cinquefoil, the form of which will hardly permit us to assign the thimble to a later epoch than c 1500. This specimen is of stout brass, ten-twelfths of an inch high; the top domed, and with the sides thickly covered with a spiral of large indentations.' A sixteenth-century thimble is also mentioned of which the top and a good part of the sides are indented and the lower part is encompassed by a band of sixteen circlets with an eleven-rayed star in each, together with another one which is very similar, but instead of the belt of stars is surrounded by the words 'God Save the Queen'—a very fashionable epigraph in Elizabethan days. Also mentioned is 'an ancient thimble dug out of the ruins of Stocks Market, with the motto, "I wis it Better", which would seem to be of the same period'.

A maker's mark appears on some of the examples already referred to in the collection at the London Museum and, in many of the later thimbles, latten has been used as well as the more common bronze or copper. During excavations in London Wall a number made of latten were found which dated from between the early sixteenth- and late seventeenth centuries.

In the Kunstgewerbemuseum in Berlin there are several examples of medieval and later thimbles, mostly German in origin. There is an interesting small bronze, acorn-shaped thimble with small indentations on it and another, gold-plated silver, with a flat top showing two heads painted under glass. This is approximately 1·9cm in height and dates from c 1580–1600. This type seems to have been popular in Germany, since there are others of the same period, one being also gold-plated silver with a flat top, but bearing a floral design covered with a transparent material which might possibly be horn. At the side is the date 1606, with the letters VGMN above. The sides of the thimble are inscribed with scroll ornament and on the lower edge is engraved 'Iunkfrau Ivstine von Herten'. Another thimble of a slightly earlier date is of copper with scroll ornament, and bears, engraved around the rim, the charming sentiment which, translated, means 'Happiness and love no thief can steal from me' and the date '1599'. Much later, but interesting as another example of a datable thimble, is one decorated with a tendril of leaves, and bearing inside four stamps: three crowns (Sweden), a crowned G (Goteborg), IDB (Johann Daniel Blomsterwall, Master, 1810–41), and the karat marking 18K. All these thimbles are from the well-known collection of A. Figdor of Vienna.

In the same museum there is another interesting specimen of the thimbles made in the shape of the famous Tailors' Guild Cup (see also page 88). It is in partly gold-plated copper, and around the edge is written 'Vivat Die Ehrsame Schneiderzunft' or 'Long Life to the Highly Esteemed Guild of Tailors'.

By the seventeenth century, silver thimbles were to be found in common use amongst the middle classes in most of Europe and were considered worthy of remark in wills and other records. In England, too, the thimble had begun to develop from being simply utilitarian into a personal possession or a special gift or momento. A French inventory of 1693 lists amongst the effects of one Claudine Bouzonnet Stella 'three silver thimbles', and there are many references to the possession of 'a silver thimble' in other inventories of the day.

French Thimbles—1700 Onwards

By the eighteenth century, in France at least there were a great number of thimbles set with all manner of precious stones, and they were adorned with a great diversity of flower sprays and motifs, chased and engraved in different coloured golds. It is to this period that some of the finest specimens in parti-coloured golds belong. And not only the precious metals, but mother-of-pearl and porcelain were materials for her thimble makers.

But the various troubles, internal revolution and external wars, which befell France during the 1700s meant that, by the beginning of the nineteenth century, precious metals there were becoming prohibitively expensive and difficult to obtain. It is not, however, for nothing that French silversmiths and jewellers are numbered amongst the finest in the world. Since gold was beyond the reach of the average customer, and since it was unpatriotic during war to display lavish ornaments, they proceeded to execute these small 'necessities of daily life' in steel, and even in iron. So great was their skill that frequently, as H. R. D'Allemagne tells us, 'the beauty of the work was ample compensation for the small value of the material employed'. A certain Sieur Dumeny of Saint Julien-du-Sault, was especially renowed for this type of work, and his name figures frequently in catalogues and lists. Even today a really fine steel thimble of this period has a very considerable value, and these items are particularly difficult to come by. In 1819 an exhibition was held in the Palais du Louvre, in which steel thimbles were shown by the firm of Rouy et Berthier, and these were stated by the judges' report on exhibits to be 'perfectly executed and of a pleasing shape, beautifully finished, and without any of the faults of thimbles in copper, gold, ivory, mother-of-pearl, and wood'.

It is also recorded that a certain Michaud Laboute, jeweller, exhibited on the same occasion, some thimbles 'of which the interior was lined with platinum whilst the exterior was of silver'. This is of particular interest, since it is the first reliable, dated, reference regarding the lining of thimbles which the writer has so far found. China thimbles sometimes have a gold, or other metal, lining, but it is in dispute as to whether this was added later or was incorporated when the thimbles were first made. During Victorian times, and in the early part of this century, it was quite usual in England to take a silver thimble which had worn thin and had prick-marks in it to any jeweller, who would run a little silver round the interior, which, when set and burnished, formed a lining and made the thimble almost as good as new. It was a common service for which only a very small charge was made, but something which very few jewellers would do these days. It seems probable from the quoted reference that the idea of lining china thimbles came in about the late 1700s or early 1800s, but it may well have had its origin in an earlier practice of re-lining worn thimbles.

At the Exhibition of French Industrial Products in 1823 there were thimbles on view known as *verges-de-fer*, which are near relatives of the great iron thimbles known in England as 'thimmel pie', or 'Dame's thimmels', with which the village school-mistress rapped the heads of inattentive pupils. Both the *verge-de-fer* and 'Dame's thimmels' might be called cousins to the type later known as 'Dorcas thimbles', which usually had an iron lining, thus making them more durable and able to stand up to heavy usage. At this exhibition also there were on display thimbles of *doublé d'argent*, and others encircled with *doublé d'or*, being of silver and gold plate respectively.

It may be as well to mention here that it was probably in either France or Italy that the first 'secret thimbles' were made. These have a loose top, which can be opened up to reveal a small inner compartment lying just under the dome of the thimble. It is interesting to speculate exactly what secrets these tiny thimbles enclosed—some secret message, some rendezvous to keep for love or war, or perhaps just the rather more prosaic cachou which our ancestors loved to suck. Unfortunately, what is mistaken for a secret compartment often contains nothing more interesting than the thread lines by means of which the thimble could be screwed on to some other article, forming a handle, or on to a chatelaine. Thread lines are also found on the inside of the base of many thimbles, for the same purpose. Some fitted on to a small etui, or sometimes screwed on to a base which thus formed a holdall for pins and needles, as in plate, page 125. The writer has found several which, amongst other things, fitted on to a corkscrew— one wonders why?

English Thimbles—1642 Onwards

In England, during the Civil War (1642–52) the great Cavalier families contributed freely towards the coffers of King Charles, cheerfully sacrificing their silverware and gold plate. But the Parliamentary forces, particularly in the later years, earned the title of the 'thimble and bodkin army', since these humble items were to be found in considerable numbers amongst the offerings of their supporters. In English literature of the seventeenth century these political gifts are a recurring theme. Pepys alludes to it in his *Diary*, 3 April 1663, mentioning that Hugh Peter's preaching during the Civil War stirred up the maids of the City to bring in their bodkins and thimbles. Howell (1594–1666) states that 'the seamstress brought in her silver thimble, the chambermaid her bodkin, and the cook her silver spoon' in his *Philanglus*. Popular ballards of the era also refer to the subject:

> And now for a fling at your thimbles,
> Your bodkins, rings and whistles,

In truck for your toys
We'll fit you with boys,
'Tis the doctrine of Hugh's Epistles!

Yet another tells us:

To pull down their King
Their plate they would bring
And other precious things;
So that Sedgwick and Peters
Were no small getters
By their bodkins, thimbles and rings.

Whatever their patriotic fervour and sentiments, their rhyming and scansion leave a lot to be desired!

It was not only in the political field that thimbles were given. In 1663 we find James Dillon, the future Lord Roscommon, sending a gift of two thimbles to Mary Verney and her cousin, Doll Leake, with an accompanying note that 'the one should not hurt a fine finger by the making of handkerchiefs, nor the other receive a prick in working my lady's buttons'. A graceful gift gracefully given.

Within the last few weeks I have been shown a gold thimble which a friend discovered whilst renewing some old wooden window-sills in her house, which dates back to the 1200s. It had obviously fallen into the crack between the wood and the masonry of the window-sill and must have lain there for some very considerable time, since no member of the family could remember ever having seen it or heard any mention of it. It is very worn and dented, but is a most charming little piece, and would appear to be late seventeenth or early eighteenth century, with traces of bevelling around the rim, and the inscription 'Tho Absent Ever Dear' combined with oak leaves in the band above the rim. When found it was so dark it looked like common metal, but polishing revealed its true nature and the lovely warm gold shone through.

In the *Journal of the British Archaeological Association* dated 1879 there is a reference to a thimble made in 'Prince Rupert's metal': 'The slightly domed top is smooth, with a ring round its margin; the upper part of the sides is indented, the lower decorated with a scroll pattern, and there is a trifling rim at the base. This thimble is really a tasteful little thing in its way.' 'Prince Rupert's metal' is more coppery in aspect than brass, and somewhat more attractive, and its invention is accredited to Prince Rupert of Cavalier fame, but it is doubtful whether he actually discovered it or whether it was so named as a compliment to him.

Often an open-topped steel thimble is lined with brass, thus strengthening it quite considerably, or a thin brass thimble may have a steel band round it with indentations to take the full pressure of the needle. There is a long list of objects stocked by a toy seller dwelling 'at the Green Parrot near Chancery Lane' in 1762 which includes 'steel topt and other thimbles'. These, clearly enough, were for the ordinary run of mortals. The ladies of quality of the eighteenth century, sitting on their silk cushions whilst they 'sewed a fine seam' had other and more delicate finger protection. Once again gold was creeping into its own, together with almost every type of material conceivable. Glass thimbles found their way over from Venice and Bohemia, porcelain and china ones came from the great pottery firms in England and the Continent, and wooden ones from Germany and Austria. France, as we have seen, until the days of her troubles produced exquisitely worked specimens in various materials.

It is a matter of regret that whilst all thimbles made before 1738 ought to have been hallmarked, this was not always the case. The regulation was never strictly adhered to, and after that date both gold and silver thimbles alike were given exemption until 1792, when it was withdrawn from silver thimbles weighing over five pennyweight. An option was retained, however, whereby manufacturers could, if they so requested, have the hallmark applied by the assay offices, thereby guaranteeing the standard of any thimbles weighing less than this. This option still holds good at the present time.

Of the more expensive thimbles of the 1700s many are extremely elegant and often, also, served a dual purpose. They are frequently combined with scent flacons, or they are found with a crest or monogram engraved on the dome or under a removable base for use as a seal. The writer can vividly remember seeing an elderly relative seal a letter by pressing her thimble into the wax. To the child it seemed an extraordinary way of making a seal-mark, since she had only seen signet or hand-stamp seals before that, but she was shown the seal incorporated in the thimble and told that it was an old custom and had once been quite a normal procedure. Sometimes a thimble screws on to a pair of scissors, or forms the base for a stiletto. The variety of combinations is endless.

A particular feature of gold and silver thimbles of the later part of the eighteenth century is the *quatre-couleur* (four-colour) work used. This is frequently found in the decoration round the lower part of the thimble, usually in the form of fruit or flowers, or grape and vine leaves, oak leaves and acorns, etc, as in the gold thimbles illustrated on page 108. The Regency period specialised in high relief work and their great silversmiths have left us a number of interesting specimens in the prominently inlaid style of the period.

It was also the day of the loveliest versions of the porcelain thimble. Most of the great houses which specialised in china and porcelain engaged in the manufacture of these tiny objects, and those which have come down to us are very lovely indeed. Sometimes the tops are steel-lined, and occasionally a strengthening band of steel, silver or gold is added round the lower portion, but on the whole they are made purely and simply in china and porcelain, with charming scenes painted on them, or sprays of flowers, clusters of fruit, or birds. In a few, the whole of the dome is made in silver or steel, but the majority of tops are in plain china with wide, bold pounce marks. A Meissen thimble of this era, no more than half an inch high and lined with gold, sold recently at Christies for 1,000 gns (£1,050). It is decorated, with incredible precision and grace, by a continuous harbour scene which features thirty figures, six bales of cotton, a large barrel and a view of some ships in the distance. It is only fair to say that both the thimble and the price are extremely rare; even for these days! So far as the thimble is concerned, these were the halcyon days of its history.

When we come to the Victorian era, seldom has such enthusiasm, industry, and productivity been equalled as was then displayed. In every field men sought to outdo all other nations and all other ages, if not always in elegance and quality, at least in

sheer outpouring of quantity. It is certain that any new collector
of thimbles will be able to accumulate literally dozens of Victorian
examples in silver without any effort at all, since silver thimbles
of the late Victorian years are obtainable by the score (see also
Chapter 10).

It is true of course that silver was so readily available in Victoria's happy reign that it was used for nearly every possible
object, and the silver table of the Victorian drawing-room, with
its display of small silverware, or 'toys', was almost *de rigueur*. Not
only the middle-class drawing-rooms boasted their display of
silver, but even the simplest homes usually had their little cabinet
containing several small pieces of silver—a christening mug,
christening spoons, a silver vase, sweetmeat dishes and baskets,
and such trinkets. Silver portrait frames, silver napkin rings, the
little Cinderella silver shoe with its blue velvet pincushion, and
silver buckles and buttons could be found in all but the very
poorest homes up and down the countryside. And practically every
workbasket in the land boasted at least one, and often more, silver
thimbles.

Unfortunately, however, the Victorians were also overfond of
gimmickry, to an extent which even our own age has hardly, as yet,
exceeded. And this applies to their thimbles also. For the most
part, those dated after 1850 or so are undistinguished and of no
great degree of workmanship. Certainly no century ever produced
more 'novelties', good, bad, and indifferent, in this particular
sphere. Souvenirs came into their own as never before or since.
There are innumerable examples engraved with views of well-
known buildings such as the Tower of London, St Paul's, London
Bridge or Buckingham Palace, and this applies not only to
London, 'the heart of the Empire', but to nearly every other city
of any considerable size. The Great Exhibition of 1861 provided a
great theme for the thimble makers, and there are many others of
a purely local character such as Brighton Pavilion, or one of the
popular spas, often engraved also with the legend 'A Present
from. . . .' The metal thimble at the bottom of page 108 has a
small hole in the dome through which, when held to the light,
views of Ipswich can be seen. Most holiday resorts sold this type
of holiday memento. Another Victorian fancy, seen in the same

photograph, is the thimble shaped in the form of a finger with the finger-nail clearly defined.

In the typically patriotic manner of the time, many bore portraits of the Queen and Prince Consort. Others give lists of the dates which every loyal citizen was expected to have engraved upon the memory—certainly on her thimble, at any rate, for learning or meditating upon whilst she sewed her sampler or her comforter:

Queen Victoria. Born May 24, 1819
Ascended the Throne. June 20, 1837
Crowned. June 28, 1838
Married Pc. Albert. Feb 10, 1840
Princess Royal born, Nov 21, 1840

On one such thimble—possibly on many others also—an inscription has been neatly added in round the rim, to bring the story up to date with true Victorian passion for accuracy: 'Christened at Buckingham Palace. Feb. 10, 1841.'

Many Victorian thimbles were made for children and are often to be found in 'sets', that is to say, several thimbles of varying sizes contained inside each other, and allowing for the growth of the small needlewoman. Such little nests of thimbles are very charming, but should not be confused with the salesmen's samples which were usually in an inferior metal and merely an indication of shape, pattern, etc. The true thimbles, when made in silver, frequently have a small motto or text on them. It was, in fact, the first trinket a little girl would own, long before she was allowed to wear personal jewellery such as a simple necklace, bracelet or brooch. Many a child's eyes must have glistened when one of the pretty thimbles we may still have today was given her. Some are charmingly engraved with stars, or flowers, some have little scenes round the base, and many have the inscription round the rim giving the name or initials of both donor and recipient.

But, for the most part, Victorian thimbles were turned out wholesale in Birmingham and other industrial centres, and dozens of these items can be collected all bearing the same formal floral decoration in bands, as an all-over pattern, or incorporated with one or other of the similar formal designs of the period. Unfortunately for the collector, in this type of thimble there is little in the way of originality or variety—which was perhaps the reason for the popularity of the 'gimmick' type of Victorian thimble rather than the ordinary everyday article.

There is an interesting illustration on page 108 where two apparently similar Italian thimbles may be seen side by side on the top line. It was indeed only by the modern version coming into her hands that the writer was able to check up on the date of the older version already in her possession. This is a simple silver thimble, with pink semi-precious stones set round the base. Most of the stones are missing, but it is nevertheless a particularly charming little item, though for some time it was not possible to check accurately on its origin or date. Then a friend visited Italy on holiday and on her return sent a little thimble as a holiday gift. The note accompanying it mentioned that this was a modern version of an old early eighteenth-century Italian design. Set down beside the little original thimble there could be no doubt about the matter. True, the modern one is of ordinary metal and the mounting round the rim is gilt, enclosing blue stones; the top is stamped with a design which must hold the world-copyright for thimble tops, since it appears on thimbles of almost all nations, but nevertheless the two thimbles are identical in design. Seldom has a holiday gift been as much appreciated as was that little turquoise-blue studded thimble from Italy.

On the bottom row of page 108 is a strange looking object unfamiliar to most of the younger generation but well enough known amongst Edwardians and their elders. This is a finger-shield, or finger-guard, and as such probably first cousin to the early British *gwniadur* and as old as the true thimble itself, though less frequently mentioned in history. Originally such guards were fashioned from horn, ivory, tortoiseshell, and similar materials for ordinary light sewing, but when used for heavy work they were made of metal, and the top part was cut sharply away diagonally so that only a narrow band at the rim was left whole, as may be seen on page 125. They were worn on the first finger of the left hand to protect the flesh from being picked up by the needle when hemming. A similar sort of guard is used in tambour work, but this is worn on the forefinger of the right hand, and there is a slight notch at the top of the guard which guides the tambour hook and also serves to press down the material until the stitch is drawn through to the surface. These are seldom used today since little tambour work is done, but finger-shields made in various forms of celluloid and plastic are still available in shops.

In itself the thimble is a very humble article—so small, so domestic that it finds no mention in the swift-moving history of the world. Nevertheless, just because it is small, it is one of the articles which can still be collected by those who cannot indulge in the more expensive *objets-d'art et vertu*, for only the very old or extremely rare versions are outside the range of the average pocket. Because of its size, also, it is one of the few things which do not demand too much space in the modern house, and can be displayed with very good effect in quite small cabinets. Certainly anyone collecting needlework boxes will want to find the loveliest and most fitting one available if the original in the box has been lost.

THIMBLE CASES

Special thimble cases have been known for centuries, but were usually only for the benefit of the more exclusive circles of society.

Sixteenth-century goldsmiths and silversmiths in France were producing thimbles in precious metals, setting them with all manner of stones, and providing them with cases and caskets at a time when the thimbles in England were very simply decorated and housed. In the inventory of the jewels and precious stones of the King of Navarre, 1583, there is a reference which reads: '*Un petit coffre de cuir noir, là où est dedans deux dés d'or à coudre, garnis de rubis. . . .*' It would indeed be interesting to be able to find these little gold thimbles set with their rubies in the little black leather casket.

Amongst the personal possessions of Queen Elizabeth I of England, preserved at Burghley House, near Stamford, there is a plain gold thimble, indented but unornamented, and an inventory of her possessions speaks of 'a nedel case of cristall, garnished with silver-gilt, with two thimbles in it'. This is the nearest thing to a thimble case she appears to have possessed and, so far as the writer can ascertain, it is unfortunately no longer in existence.

Thimbles and Thimble Cases

Most thimble cases which are likely to be available to the collector today are of eighteenth- or nineteenth-century manufacture, but within that short space of time there is a wide choice. They have been made in the widest variety of materials and shapes, ranging from horn, ivory, vegetable ivory or corozo nut, polished woods, glass, shagreen, leathers, tortoiseshell and china, right up the range of fine materials to the richly ornamented agates, marbles and jades decorated with gold and silver and enamels of the Fabergé period. Acorns have always been especial favourites for housing thimbles, but walnuts, strawberries, apples, and all manner of other fruits were also popular. Eggs, also, in every sort of material, abound, together with small barrels, egg-cups, chalices and simple cylindrical boxes. In the middle of the nineteenth century small caskets similar to ring boxes, in leather or velvet, were fashionable forms, and baskets in fine wickerwork or realistically carved in wood or ivory are also frequently found. As with many other Victorian articles, thimble cases were frequently sold as souvenirs, usually in polished light wood cases, with black-and-white pictures on the lid depicting Gloucester Cathedral, Glastonbury Tor, Osborne House, or other such favourite spots. Sometimes they housed not only a thimble, but also a yard measure and an emery, or else a wax-holder, and such containers should perhaps strictly be called sewing boxes. Various examples of thimble cases and wax holders may be seen in the plate on page 125.

At the height of the power and luxurious living of the Imperial Russian Court, small Easter-egg caskets were particularly favoured. Some of these, especially those made by Fabergé and his workmen, are exquisite, being enamelled in a range of unusual shades, and richly ornamented with silver and gold tracery and embellished with precious stones.

CHAPTER 6

SCISSORS AND STILETTOS

SCISSORS

No workbox worth its name is complete without at least one pair of scissors—many have more.

Few words have had such a variety of spellings through the centuries as our simple word 'scissors'. Frequently, in old literature, it is almost unrecognisable, having varied from sissoures, sysers, sizzors, cysowre, cizars, cissours, scissours and many others down to our present form. The 'sc' appears to be due to an etymologising confusion between the original Latin *cisorium* which meant simply a cutting instrument, and the verb *scindere*, to cut, split off, or to rend. There is no evidence of this confusion earlier than the sixteenth century, though in English medieval literature scissor, cissor, or cisor was the common word for a tailor. The distinction between shears and scissors appears to be that the larger types, especially those which cannot be manipulated with one hand alone, are commonly known as shears, and are sometimes worked by a spring action, whereas the smaller types, with pivoted blades held together by a single screw, are classed as scissors. Tailors refer to the larger sizes as shears, the medium size as trimmers, and the smaller ones as scissors or cuts.

Some of the earliest forms known to us resemble sugar tongs or tweezers more than anything else—it is difficult, in fact, to associate them with any sort of cutting action whatsoever. Both the tweezer and the pivotal types are known to have been made of iron in ancient times, but it is probable that the blades were made of steel where any form of cutting was in question, since steel was known long before the Roman era. The pivotal types are mentioned frequently from medieval times onwards in various spelling forms, but nearly always the trimming of beards and hair seems to be referred to rather than the cutting of materials. In a reference in 1384 Chaucer makes this clear:

> And moo berdys in two oures withoute Rasour or Sisoures
> Y-made then greyndes be of sondes.

In Beryn, 1400, we find a similar type of reference: 'Getith a pair of sissours, sherith my berd a-noon', and as late as the seventeenth century most mentions of scissors refer to the same usage:

> 'The haire on his chin . . . he used almost
> daily to cut it with his sizers.'
>
> Moryson
>
> 'He . . . had neither money enough to hire
> a Barber, nor to buy sizars . . .'
>
> Cowley

The pair of seventeenth-century scissors in their leather sheath shown on page 126 might well have been used for this type of service, and may explain the reason for the continued existence of the tweezer type long after the pivotal form had shown its obvious advantages for tailoring. The scissors in the photograph could conceivably be used as a form of razor but it is difficult to imagine this being effectively achieved by the pivotal types. However, in a play of 1483, *Richard III*, Act 1, we find a hint of the usage which is more familiar to us: 'No merchant Stranger . . . shall bring into this Realm . . . tailors shears, sysors. . . .'

French inventories from 1306 onwards make mention of scissors, but for the most part they are in precious metals. Charles VI possessed several such items:

1389 2 silver-gilt scissors from the forge of Clermont, the handles being of 2CC and the screw in the form of a crown

1401 To William Turel, gentleman of the Wardrobe, to the Queen for silver which Madam gave him for a pair of scissors of Toulouse, for tailoring the garments of Madame . . . 36 Parisien sous.

The reputation of the town of Moulins was solidly established on the Continent by the sixteenth century, and we find that the royal nails were trimmed by scissors made there:

1560 For a pair of scissors, of Moulin manufacture, garnished with copper-gilt, for trimming the nails of M. the King.

From the Middle Ages onwards scissors began to take various forms according to the different sorts of work on which they were to be employed, but France still led the industry. There is mention of scissor smiths in the register of the newly formed Cutlers' Company in England in 1624, but it was nearly a century before English scissors began to compete seriously with those of Continental manufacture.

There is an interesting Flemish tapestry of the Tournai School in the Victoria & Albert Museum, London, of a pastoral entitled 'la main chaude', and which dates from the early sixteenth century. This depicts men and women busy at their various tasks at sheepshearing time, and all of them carry, attached to rings on their waistbands or girdles, large pairs of scissors, or small shears, together with various other small personal articles such as combs, daggers, reed-pipes, etc, and small squarish-shaped boxes in which they carried what might be called a 'first-aid kit' of mendicants and special things needed at this particular season. These little boxes only appear in pastoral scenes showing events connected with sheep-shearing, but are an interesting item for us since they are believed to have included needles and twine amongst their contents. Possibly these latter were used to mend cuts, but more probably were needed for sewing up the sacks into which the fleece was put.

The scissors shown, however, are our immediate interest. They would appear to be about 10in long and very strongly made: little different, in fact, from the tailors' shears or the pinking shears of our own time—heavy handled, strong bladed and with sloping, blunted ends. It would seem that the fine pointed ends we associate with scissors only came into being as needlework and embroidery progressed and became more commonplace.

By the eighteenth century, however, English scissors were considered to be superior to those of French manufacture, although by this time Spanish craftsmen were also making beautifully damascened scissors elaborately decorated on both handles and blades, and often gilded and painted. Italy and Germany were likewise turning out fine scissors. In *Les Accessoires Du Coutume et du Mobilier* there are some fine examples of these types of scissors, from the collections of H. R. D'Allemagne and of A. Figdor, but there would appear to have been few of these more elaborate examples in England. A type of Spanish scissor which was apparently fairly common in England is shown on page 126. These are late eighteenth century, and vary in length from about 6in to 9in, usually being etched on steel as a form of decoration, or damascened in gold or silver.

Strange and fantastic styles were also much in vogue, but usually in the Near and Far East. The pelican-type bird scissors (plate, page 126) probably come from Persia, and it is difficult to see exactly what purpose they could have fulfilled. The back lifts up slightly as the finger is inserted into the handle-piece, and the beak opens sideways, the eye of the bird being formed by the screw. The blades, however, are slightly hollow, and not particularly sharp, so unless these were a 'toy' in the old sense, and merely desk-scissors for paper cutting or opening letters, they would appear to be singularly impracticable.

The long, slender blade depicted just below them in the same plate, is an interesting example of how very varied scissors are in style. These scissors, too, are Persian, and they also have hollowed blades. When closed, they fit together to form the dagger-like instrument shown in the picture. The handles are carefully fashioned to fit finger and thumb, and the joint where they open can be seen in the photograph around the more elongated of the two finger holds. They are normally classified as desk-scissors, and the single-bladed style seems to accord well with use as a letter opener. The writer was, however, puzzled by the hollow blades, even though one day she learned that such scissors were frequently worn tucked down the side of the leg, much as in the manner of the Scottish dirk, or *skean-dhu* (the black knife) which formed such a useful secret weapon in the early days of the wars against Scotland, until the English discovered where it was concealed. In their present connection, although these scissors would certainly form a useful surprise weapon, the hollow blades still seemed unnecessary and somewhat singular, until in *Les Accessoires du Coutume et du Mobilier* a passage came to light stating that the sages amongst the Turks and Persians had used this type of scissor for cutting the little triangles of paper on which they wrote their *lettres missives*. This puts a different complexion on the matter, and after inquiry

Page 107 (left) *Russian 16th-century chatelaine in gold and enamel, with needlecase, scissors and thimble in case; (below) silver needlecase, first half of the 19th century, with fluting and scrollwork*

Page 108 (top row) *Five silver thimbles: Victorian, 19th century Viennese, William IV, Italian c 1700 and modern Italian copy;*

(2nd row) Victorian silver thimble; early 1800s gold with amethyst top and particoloured gold flowers in relief, another gold ditto with fine ivy leaf ornament, two mid-Victorian silver;

(3rd row) silver thimble, ditto with non-slip lining, child's, two of a nest of three and mid-Victorian thimble;

(4th row) cellulose finger shield, nickel 'finger nail' thimble, brass, horn and another brass, the latter with peep-show in top, all Victorian

it was possible to see how important the hollow blades really were in certain operations. The term *lettres missives* usually denotes a diplomatic or political message of a secret nature, but can also be used, in a lighter vein, for clandestine love notes. These scissors must therefore often have played a vital part in the affairs (and *affaires*) of the day. The small triangular slips containing the vital message were put into the cavity of the blades, which were then closed, and the 'dagger' was slipped down the side of the leg garments or straps where, under the flowing robes of Eastern garments, it was completely hidden. Even if the carrier was captured or questioned, the secret hiding place was not likely to be known, especially to the 'infidels', and the secret message was safe.

But, in the more prosaic world of the West, such Arabian Night adventures played little part in the development of the common scissors which continued to be much as they had been for centuries—a cross-shape with two rings for the handles, gradually becoming slightly more elaborately decorated as time went by, but otherwise very little different from the earliest pivoted types of Roman days.

However, as fine embroidery, cut-work and various forms of lace-work came into fashion, so scissors had to become finer and more delicately fashioned and, by the eighteenth century, Continental scissor smiths began to find new forms and methods of manufacture. Many of the smaller types are excessively elaborate, with intricate designs on the handles gradually increasing in complexity; but eventually the increasing delicacy of the tracery work used seems to have become too frail to bear much strain, and it is quite difficult to find good examples which are not broken or otherwise damaged. In very many eighteenth- and nineteenth-century workboxes the fitting for the scissors is either empty or the original pair has been replaced by later, non-matching scissors.

By Victorian days, even the medium sized pairs of scissors in ordinary household use had begun to be ornamented, instead of being severely plain as in previous centuries. Scissors used in the kitchen were still obviously utilitarian, but sewing shears or scissors were frequently enlivened by a little ornamentation, usually by way of scrollwork, and were less severely practical. Victorian scissors may, in fact, often be recognised by the more elongated shape of the handles, instead of the earlier, ring-shaped ones, together with the frequent appearance of the scrollwork just mentioned either on the handles themselves, or round the juncture of the blade and handle. The small scissors fitted into workboxes continued to be dainty and ornamental, the handles often chased with fruit and foliage, as those in the workbox on page 18, or made of mother-of-pearl, or ivory, or with the blades forming the beak of a stork, or other bird, such as is still popular today. In Germany these stork scissors often include the traditional baby carried in a sling. The earlier, ring-type handles, can be seen in the mother-of-pearl scissors in the casket on page 71.

But, increasingly, new forms came into being as special aids to different types of embroidery. Sometimes small scissors are found which have a protuberance at the end of one of the blade-points, as though a lump of metal had dropped on to it and not been filed off. These are lace-scissors, and were particularly used for Carrick-macross lace, where the design is formed by cutting away the top layer of material from the underlying layer of net. The beautiful lacy pattern so much admired is thus achieved only by great delicacy and precision, so the ordinary small embroidery scissors were not entirely satisfactory. The small 'bump' at the tip of the new type of scissor helped to keep the two layers of materials carefully separated and lessen the risk of a false cut.

Buttonhole scissors are also sometimes found in old workboxes, but these are comparative newcomers to the family of cutting implements, and a Victorian invention. They may be distinguished by the small screw protruding at the handle-end of the blades, which determined the size of the buttonhole to be cut. One such pair may be seen in the photograph on page 126. Before the invention of these scissors, buttonholes had had to be cut, either by folding the material when a large-sized hole was being worked, or by using a small implement sometimes found in old, fitted cases, known as a buttonhole cutter or seam-knife. This is a small tool, usually some 3 to 4in long, with a bone or other type of handle and a sharp, slightly spade-shaped blade. Anyone who has tried to cut a buttonhole with one knows that, apart from its use on fine silks and very thin materials, it was not the ideal tool. Nevertheless it was all they had in those days. It was more frequently

14 *Typical scissor cases of 17th and 18th centuries, usually in metal
or in leather. Approx 4–5in*

known as a seam-knife, for it was used both for cutting the
stitches when unpicking seams and for pressing seams open to
enable them to lie flat.

By the beginning of the nineteenth century the cutter was

III

largely superseded by a small folding, or pocket, knife which was used not only for sewing but also for sharpening quills used in writing, whence it derives its modern name of 'penknife'. These small folding knives are very frequently found in old French etuis of the eighteenth-century and in mid-nineteenth-century workboxes.

Since the smaller scissors were originally carried at the waist with other toilet and sewing accessories, many of them had cases for their protection, and these are often extremely richly orna-mented. An inventory of 1599 speaks of two gold etuis for holding scissors, one garnished with diamonds and the other with rubies and diamonds. Most of these scissor cases were in solid iron finely engraved and chased, or in pierced and engraved iron, and many were intricately damascened or made in richly tooled leathers (diagram, page 111). During the eighteenth century the cases were often in pierced steel, but young ladies of fashion were beginning to use small boxes of sandalwood garnished with steel, either in flat or in spirally turned styles. From this time onwards, sheaths protecting the points of the scissors came into vogue, and there are many examples of these available made in ivory, gold, silver, richly tooled and gilded leather and other materials as well as steel. Even in fitted workboxes of the early Victorian period, scissors are frequently found with small sheaths protecting the slender blade-points, as in the ones shown on page 143.

The difference in form between the scissor handles in the early eighteenth-century workbox on page 89 and those of the nine-teenth century (plate, page 72) can be clearly seen and comparison may be made between the old X-shaped scissors with ring-handles attached, and the later type where the finger-grips 'flow' more easily in a graceful line down to the blades. Even later, they were shaped separately to fit finger and thumb.

STILETTOS

Stilettos—small, dagger-like implements with a handle and finely pointed blade—were an integral part of every workbox. They were used mainly for unpicking stitches, for stabbing holes or eyelets, or for pricking or pouncing, whereby a pattern is transferred to the material with the aid of a pounce-pad containing white chalk or fine graphite powder. Indeed, even today, for really intricate designs, there is no satisfactory substitute. The drawing is traced on to fine, but strong, tracing paper, and then pricked all along the lines with a fine needle. The prick-marks have to be close together, forming a line, but not joining together, or the pouncing powder tends to smear. The paper has to be pinned carefully on to the material, and the fabric has to be on a firm, flat surface. Then the pounce-pad is rubbed carefully along each line so that the powder penetrates each prick-mark. When the design is complete—and it takes a considerable time if it is a large and complicated one—the paper is removed and the lines should show up clearly on the fabric. This enables the embroideress to begin to do the final transference, which may be, according to the type of work, either by working neat tacking stitches along each pounced line, or, more usually, by painting in the lines with a special ink. When this is perfectly dry, the process is complete, and work may at last begin. For a really good and detailed description of the full process, the reader could do no better than refer to Miss Beryl Dean's book *Ecclesiastical Embroidery* or her *Church Embroidery*.

As with so many other implements, stilettos were worn suspended from the girdle in the days before workboxes were in common use, and therefore they are often accompanied by an ornamental sheath. Many have very elaborate and finely decorated handles made of ivory, gold, silver, mother-of-pearl or various hardstones, and in some the blade or point is reversible and screws upwards into the handle-piece. The blades vary from the finest Spanish steel, sharp as a dagger and just about as dangerous if mishandled, to ivory, depending on the use to which the implement was to be put. Some examples may be seen on pages 89 and 144, the former showing an old steel stiletto with a flat end for seam pressing, and the latter a small Victorian ivory stiletto. For scissors and stilettos, as used in parfilage, see page 142.

CHAPTER 7

OTHER NEEDLES, TAMBOUR AND CROCHET HOOKS, SHUTTLES

KNITTING NEEDLES

Though rare indeed, and hardly recognisable because of their simple shape, the earliest knitting needles were probably of bone. Examples of clothing and wall pictures of the ancient world indicate that knitting was a firmly established craft in the Near East probably before, but certainly in the years immediately following, the death of Christ. It was used not only for clothing, but also for wall hangings, carpets and furnishings, and since any craft takes a considerable time to develop and flourish to such a peak of perfection, we can be fairly certain that it had a long-standing history for many centuries before that time.

There are some interesting facts about knitting in R. J. Forbes's excellent book, *Studies in Ancient Technology*. Amongst those mentioned is the place occupied by knitting in relation to plaiting and weaving. Amongst the finds at Dura Europos, in Mesopotamia, and also at Karanis, in Egypt, which yielded material dating from AD 38 to the seventh century, are a number of instances of knitting, and it is evident that those engaged in this work had reached a high degree of skill. The Arabs, we know, were expert in the art and it is interesting to note, in this connection, that it is often amongst people who are constantly on the move that knitting is most frequently to be found, and amongst whom it reaches its highest attainments. This may be largely because it is one of the few textile occupations which can be carried on whilst walking or riding, as is evidenced by the fact that through all centuries both men and women have been known to knit whilst herding their flocks, walking to market, watching over their cooking, and doing other domestic chores.

I am greatly indebted to Mr G. C. Boon, FSA, for being privileged to mention his find of the first Roman bronze knitting needle ever recognised. This was found in 1864–78, at Silchester, and was in the reserves at Reading Museum where Mr Boon only recently identified it. Some 29·2cm long, of a maximum of 0·3cm diameter, it runs out to rounded points at both ends. In modern terms, therefore, the gauge is about a No 11 needle. A fuller description and details will be given in Mr Boon's book, now in preparation, on Romano remains at Silchester.

Strange though it may seem to us, knitting was originally a masculine occupation, probably because of its Oriental source, and right down to the last years of the Middle Ages we find it was still so. Weaving was the occupation more usual to woman. It was not only garments such as shirts, coats, cloaks and mantles which were knitted, but also carpets, many of them being of extremely complicated design and containing a wide range of colours. It is possible that chain-link mail, which came to us from the East, owes something of its origin to the texture of knitting to which its inventors were accustomed.

By the sixteenth century, however, knitting was becoming a more normal occupation amongst women of the middle and even upper classes, and was to a certain extent taking over from weaving. But it is only about early Georgian times that we find sets of fine steel knitting needles making their appearance in bodkin, netting-needle cases, and the early flat workcases carried in the pocket. Serious knitting of garments had not at that stage come into vogue amongst the upper classes, and these very slender knitting needles were used mainly for making small purses, bags, garters, etc, and for the bead knitting which was so fashionable for a short time. From the early eighteenth century onwards a fashion arose for knitting lacy patterns in fine white threads. Instead of using ordinary lace, collars, fichus, mittens, doyleys and small cloths were all knitted in the most delicate and lacelike of patterns, which called for needles of so fine a gauge that they were hardly thicker than ordinary sewing needles. Some of these can still be found in workboxes in knitting-needle cases and other containers, and may be recognised by the fact that they are very often coloured blue across the centre to help the knitter see the fine white stitches against what would otherwise be the confusing silver-white of the needle.

During Victorian times knitting gradually assumed the forms with which it is associated today. Consequently knitting needles found in nineteenth-century workboxes, whether fitted or unfitted are, on the whole, fairly commonplace ones and made of steel, bone, ivory and tortoiseshell. For the most part, however, the knitting needles which are part of the fittings of a needlework box are of the smaller, finer varieties used for small articles; the larger, heavier and longer types were usually kept in special receptacles apart from the workbox.

NETTING NEEDLES

From knitting tools we now turn our attention to netting needles and the other implements allied to them.

Netting is so ancient a craft that it is impossible to know when or where it was first practised. Most primitive races have used nets for fishing and for hunting, and so mankind has from earliest days been conversant with the art. In later centuries nets were found to be useful for a wider range of purposes, and in the period with which we are more immediately concerned, garden nets, containers, bags, purses, fichus, shawls, gloves and many other articles, small and large, were made of netting in different thicknesses and styles. With our modern ease of purchasing almost any item in a shop or through a mail order catalogue, we overlook the fact that right up to the Victorian era almost all domestic articles in a household were homemade in one sense or another, except perhaps in the very wealthiest households.

The first netting was probably made by using a simple shuttle with a V-shaped notch at either end and a short wooden gauge. But in time, as finer meshes were required a finer implement became necessary, and the netting needle was introduced. This was a much longer, thinner, instrument than the original shuttle making for more ease in handling, with a large eye at either end, and usually made from iron, bone, or wood. In the East, netting had reached a high degree of perfection even before the dawn of the Christian era, and had developed in so many diverse directions that it is not always recognised as such, the finest of gossamer-like veiling being, in fact, network. Over the centuries it gradually developed also into the form of lace work which we term needle lace.

As the term implies, netting needles are basically in the shape of a needle—long and slender, but with the ends flattened or spatulated and divided into fork-like prongs. The thread was wound from one prong down the blade to the other prong and then back again, until the needle was full and ready for use. Such needles vary in length according to the fineness of the work to be undertaken, some being 8 to 10in long, and varying down to about 3 to 4in. In many instances they are made of bone, horn, ivory, or tortoiseshell, and even more frequently they are made of wood. Netting needles are not usually found in very valuable materials such as gold, or mother-of-pearl, or very fancifully carved. The slender nature of the needle and the amount of constant movement involved probably made these materials and ornamentation impracticable.

For each variety of network different sets and different thicknesses of tools were needed. Also used was a mesh or spool, similar to a knitting needle and usually pointed at each end, which was a gauge on which the loops were made so that they were all of one size and easily slipped off. A flat ruler-like tool with a groove along one side is also often found, and this was for making the fringes which frequently were used as a finish for certain network articles. A similar tool was used for sewing up the long wallet purses which were once so popular.

The more expensive netting sets were kept in cylindrical cases similar to, but somewhat larger than, the old needlecases, as in the Chinese ivory netting case (plate, page 53). Eastern netting-needle cases were made of metal, ivory, or fine tooled leather, and sometimes of sandalwood and cedar, but in the West there were also special types of boxes for the various forms of network. These contained the shuttles, gauges and various other netting necessities, but many were too large to be conveniently included in a workbox and so were kept separately. Workboxes of the late eighteenth and nineteenth centuries often have a roller and ratchet fitted into a compartment, as may be seen in the box on page 89. The foundation loop in netting has to be attached to something firm and steady against which it can be pulled taut to begin the foundation of the work, and the rollers in these boxes were used for netting and for some types of lace work. Sometimes they were also used for tambour work, instead of a separate spool-knave or reel-holder, and then the roller was released and allowed to revolve in order to let the silk run freely.

True netting boxes are sometimes found which are 9 to 10in long and about 4 or 5in wide, and which contain the shuttles, or needles, and gauges, together with the necessary roller for the work. This will usually have a slit or hole through which the foundation loop may be affixed, and a handle which enables the work to be wound up to a convenient length for ease in working. Usually these boxes were used for the larger types of net work, whilst the small roller contained in so many workboxes was mainly used for working smaller articles, particularly the netting purses so popular for holding sovereigns safely (sometimes called 'thumb purses'), and the edgings and insertions which were so widely used on both clothing and domestic linen.

The study of social history often shows that, because of lack of communication, the usage made of any particular implement varied from place to place, largely because at some time or other one ingenious member of a family had discovered a particular use for an object and had handed down his use to following generations. This is certainly true of the contents of workboxes. One family will insist that a spool was used for network, whilst another will remember that great-grandmother always used it when doing crochet work. It is probably true to say that many such implements were used for whatever purpose was found most suitable by different individuals doing different types of work in different parts of the country.

TAMBOUR HOOKS

In the eighteenth century, tambour work was greatly in vogue, especially in France. Originally it was worked on a drum-shaped frame, *tambour* being the French for a drum, and the much later, simple round frames, with or without a stand, are often known as tambours even today. In this style of work the right hand holds the hook above the frame, in a more or less vertical position, and the left hand guides the thread underneath the frame. The resultant appearance of the work is similar to that of chain stitch. It was usual to use a thimble of a special type for this sort of work—an open-ended thimble which had a deep notch in it at the centre front. The needle had to be kept in the notch and guided down by means of it. Such a thimble was not essential, but was helpful, though it was added as an accessory probably only about the middle of the eighteenth century. The tambour hook itself consisted either of a handle and hook all in one piece or, more usually, of a handle into which the steel hook was fitted, a small wing nut holding it in position. The handle is slightly broadened at one end in order to ensure a firm grip, and is frequently also a container holding the long, fine blades of the hooks, or tambour needles, when not in use. Usually a point protector is screwed on over the actual hook when not in use and, when work was being done, this screwed on to the top part of the handle. Some early tambour hooks are very elaborately decorated, especially the early French eighteenth-century ones; but the types available to most collectors today will be those of the late eighteenth and nineteenth centuries, and usually made in ivory, bone or metals. An example of one of these tambour hooks may be seen on page 72 towards the forefront of the casket.

Tambour work was a pleasant pastime, and some very fine embroidery could be executed by this means, but it had the disadvantage of having to be done in a frame which limited the number of occasions on which it could be worked. On the other hand, knotting, netting, tatting and crochet could all be taken about with the minimum of inconvenience and brought out at odd moments and in almost any place, without needing the space or the disturbance involved by work on a frame. It was largely because of this that they finally superseded tambour work amongst those moving in fashionable circles, and its general decline amongst the ordinary people was due largely to the invention of machinery, in 1807, which could turn out similar styles of embroidery at much greater speeds.

Apart from tambour hooks themselves, reel-holders or spool-knaves (diagram, below) also belonged originally to tambour work, though later on, when their original work had fallen out of favour, were often used for other purposes. Many of the more elaborate ones have their own fitted cases, and some workboxes have a tambour-spool amongst their fittings, as on page 36.

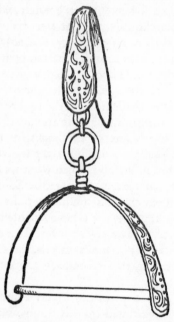

15   *Reel-holder, or spool-knave, in metal*

Reel-holders are usually stirrup-shaped, with a short chain and a clasp which fitted on to the embroideress's waist. The spindle, or bar, of the 'stirrup' enabled the spool of thread to revolve freely so that the embroideress could manipulate it easily with her left hand under the frame whilst the right hand, above the frame, controlled the tambour hook. When tambour work went out of fashion, many of these spool-knaves were used for knitting, and sometimes for crochet, although for neither were they as essential as for their original form of work.

CROCHET HOOKS

When, in the early nineteenth century, crochet became the popular handicraft, tambour hooks were frequently simply diverted from their original purpose and used for the new *crochet en air*, as it was called in France. Crochet had probably been known in the East for as long as knitting and seems to have derived from it, since there is a form of work known as Tunisian crochet, which is done with a long, straight hook very similar to a knitting needle, but with a knob at one end. The elegant art of crochet which came into being in France however is more allied to tambour work than to this, or to any form of knitting.

Early types of crochet hooks, such as we may justifiably hope to find today, are very similar to tambour hooks, that is, they are normally composed of two parts—the handle, and the steel hooks which fitted into it. Like tambour hooks, many of the earlier ones contain a hollow interior holding up to five or six metal hooks of different sizes. Gradually the wing nut of the tambour handle became unnecessary, largely because of the different angle at which a crochet hook was held, and a simple metal fitting only was necessary into which the hook slotted. Then, finally, the handle and hook were made in one piece, the handle being of matching material to the fitments of the workbox, usually in mother-of-pearl, ivory, polished woods, silver or bone. A mother-of-pearl crochet hook of this type is to be seen in the bottom right-hand corner on page 144. Finally the form we now know came into existence, probably somewhere about the early 1800s, being made all in one piece of the same material throughout, and usually in ivory, bone or eventually in steel. Examples of ivory crochet hooks may be seen on pages 35 and 144.

Special cases for crochet hooks began to be used in the mid-nineteenth century, being made sometimes in leather, shagreen, silver and other precious metals or other materials, but they are not easy to find, and were probably never very much in vogue. The Victorians used more the little handmade pouches and hussifs which so greatly rejoiced their souls and proved such an outlet for their creativity in needlework. An example of one such late-Victorian crochet-hook case, the interior of which is lined with purple velvet, may be seen on page 89.

KNOTTING AND TATTING SHUTTLES

With regard to knotting and tatting, both of these are done with the aid of one, or sometimes two, shuttles, and are allied to the old form of weaving rather than to knitting. The word 'shuttle' itself is very old, almost prehistoric in fact, coming down from the earliest forms of speech as *skutil* or, in late Old English *scytel*, and signifying a dart, harpoon, missile or arrow. In some languages the shuttle takes its name from its likeness to a boat, as in Latin *navicula*, in German *weberschiff*, or in French *navette*, by which name it is still sometimes known in England, although 'shuttle' is far more common.

In the eighteenth century, shuttles were in great demand since knotting became an essential part of any fashion-conscious woman's accomplishments. There is no particular skill in it, since it is very largely a matter of simple but rhythmic action. Its great attraction lay in the fact that it gave ample opportunity for the grace and elegance of the knotter's hands to be constantly demonstrated as she industriously plied her shuttle. Little concentration is needed for plain knotting, tatting, or crochet work, and a conversation may be carried on without distraction, so that these forms of work were excellent ways for a woman to employ both her time and her hands to advantage. We need to remember that in the days of the great courts of Europe, literally hours might be spent in just sitting around awaiting the royal pleasure or the royal appearance, and it was customary for ladies to take some needlework or embroidery with them to the many salons they attended, so that the time spent there might not be entirely fruitless or too irksome. Highly skilled embroidery would have been impossible in such circumstances, but knotting and tatting were the ideal answer.

The knotting shuttle is formed of two oval blades pointed at both ends and joined in the middle. Many of the earliest ones of the early and mid-1700s are extremely beautiful, being real works of art and made in mother-of-pearl, carved ivory, tortoiseshell, jet, pierced steel, filigree gold and silver or enamels. They were a most acceptable gift to the ladies of the period. In 1767, Mrs Delany, the writer of the famous *Letters* informs us that 'Mrs. Jeffrys has bought me a very elegant shuttle for two guineas'—a considerable sum in those days—and a few years later a Mrs Ravaud, writing to the same Mrs Delany says: 'I want to know if the inclosed knotting is what you would have it. . . . Its merit . . . is entirely owing to the instrument with which it is fabricated, the non-pareille shuttle of singular device. . . .' Less expensive, but more likely to be available to the average collector, are the shuttles of porcelain, lacquer, wood painted and veneered or decorated with straw-work, or in plain ivory, horn and bone.

The early eighteenth-century knotting shuttles are much longer than those of later years, being sometimes nearly 5in long. They also have a larger space between their tips than have the later versions, since they carried more voluminous materials such as silk cords, coarser threads and linens; those fashionable in the Courts of the mid and latter part of the century are very much finer, the tips being closer together. The shape was important, as a good shuttle contributed greatly to more perfect execution of the work.

From these evolved the tatting shuttle, which is considerably smaller, being about 2¾in by ¾in, and the name tatting, or 'tatters', originally denoted the more fragile and disjointed nature of the work. The French still call it *frivolité*, whilst the Italians call it *occhi* because of the eye-like effect of the many rings of which it is composed. In the East it is known as *makouk*, from the shuttle used to effect the work.

Together with tatting shuttles there is often found a small metal object somewhat resembling a hairpin. This may be in gold, silver or baser metals, and is a tatting pin, needed for the more elaborate patterns where picots of different sizes were made. Some tatting pins of the hairpin variety have a metal band across the middle portion, but these are usually of later Victorian manufacture. The earlier ones have no connecting band, but are sometimes found attached to a short piece of chain ending in a ring. This was worn on the left thumb, so that the tatting pin could be picked up with the right hand as required and then dropped again when no longer in use. A plain pin, some 2in long, is also found with tatting shuttles, and particularly in special tatting boxes. This is a purlin pin, also sometimes called a tatting pin, and again was a gauge for making all the picots identical in size.

In time a different method of working was devised which involved the use of two shuttles, and there are still small fitted boxes containing their pair of shuttles, purling or tatting pins, and room for the thread and work.

Page 125 (above) Thimbles. Top line: ivory, silver finger protector, Diamond Jubilee, Victorian silver, gilded bronze with Gothic lettering round base, possibly early 1700s, openwork filigree, late 18th century. Bottom row: medieval, late 18th-century child's, 19th-century polished horn with screw on base, iron and brass medieval; (below) top line: four 19th-century thimble cases, in wood and horn; bottom line: mid-Victorian ebony and ivory chalice type with silver thimble with red stone top, acorn shaped ivory thimble case with thimble, probably late 1800s, polished bone painted needlecase with silver thimble inside, and wooden wax-holder, late Victorian

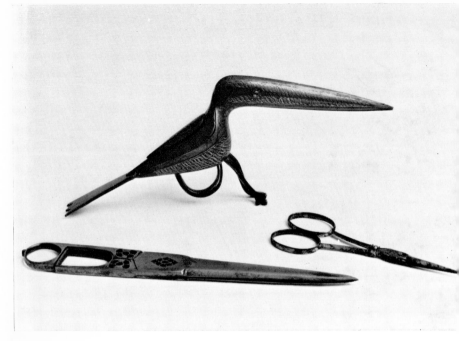

Page 126 (above) *Desk scissors, probably Persian, in form of a pelican, about mid 19th century; Persian dagger-shaped steel scissors with hollow blades, pierced decoration and engraving; pair of early 18th-century steel scissors; (below) Spanish, late 18th-century scissors, steel with gilded and etched decoration; Victorian buttonhole scissors; pair spring-type scissors and a similar 17th-century pair with leather sheath*

CHAPTER 8

MISCELLANEOUS ACCESSORIES

THREAD WINDERS AND HOLDERS

Tucked away somewhere in nearly all workboxes from about 1720 onwards there will nearly always be one or other of the forms of thread-winder which were a necessity of sewing and embroidery in earlier days; a necessity because, after the days when each household spun its own thread, silks, cottons and wools were all bought in skeins or hanks. Before use, therefore, they had to be wound on to some article which kept the thread untwisted and clean, and from which it could be taken as required. Thread-winders were the answer. They are small, flat objects, with a series of points which enabled the silk or other thread to be wound crosswise between them. They may be square-shaped, slightly rounded, rectangular, or star-shaped, and with the points or prongs set at different angles and in different styles. They vary from under 1in diameter for fine silks, to about 2in for heavier weights of thread, and late nineteenth-century boxes may sometimes contain winders 3 to 4in diameter and which were used for thick silks and for wools. Winders were made in wood, ivory, mother-of-pearl, bone, glass, straw-work and horn, and they continued to be used for silks down to the beginning of the present century; many are still in use today. For certain types of embroidery threads nothing better has yet been devised, and the more elegant types, with their coloured silks wound on them, still make a very pretty show in any box and are used by many professional needlewomen.

The beginning of the nineteenth century saw multiple winders being fitted into many boxes. They had been used earlier, but now became a regular fitment and were usually between 3 and 4in long. They consisted of a spindle which was divided into three or four compartments for holding different threads, and they were usually fitted into a special compartment. One of these multiple winders may be clearly seen fitted across the centre compartment of the Chinese box on page 36 and others can be seen in some of the other illustrations.

16 *Some different types of cotton barrels*

The really keen collector will probably wish to furnish his workbox with at least one cotton barrel (diagram, above) if not more, unless he is fortunate enough to have a fitted box which has not lost its original set. Cotton barrels date from about the end of the eighteenth century and, as the name indicates, are in the shape of a small barrel, usually in bone or ivory, though occasionally in wood or even porcelain. Inside the barrel is the small spindle which holds the thread when wound, and the top of the spindle fits through a hole in the screw-on type lid of the barrel and acts as a tiny handle. At the side of the barrel there is a small hole through which the thread is drawn out for use, and it can be wound back on to the reel by means of the protruding spindle when not needed. A simple example of an ivory cotton barrel may be seen on page 143. Less usual, and also rather less elegant perhaps, are the cotton barrels which have small handles attached to the top of the spindle. In some cases also, the lid of the barrel itself turns the reel inside and there is no protruding spindle. The ivory barrels are usually turned, or have some form of decoration, and are about an inch high, though many of the wooden ones are very considerably larger, and were probably used in the domestic quarters of large houses where the plain sewing and the hemming of linen, curtains, covers and suchlike required larger containers which would need refilling less frequently.

It could be said that we owe our present reels of cottons and silks to these early cotton barrels, since the manufacturers saw in them a new opening and began to sell their wares on spindles or, eventually, spools, which had the number and colour printed on a label round the spindle. Thus, when the spool was empty it was simply taken out of the barrel and sent back to the makers to be refilled. Cotton barrels did not last long, as we measure time today, only from about the end of the eighteenth century and through the first decade or so of the nineteenth, but they were actually a most excellent way of keeping threads clean and unentangled, and in many respects the evolution of the cotton barrel into the modern form of reel represents a loss.

So far as the manufacturer was concerned, it was cheaper and easier to make bone and ivory reels, rather than spindles for thread. Once again the manufacturer's name and the number of the thread was affixed to the shank of the reel so it could be returned for refilling when necessary. These reels were often carved on the top, and sometimes had a little screw-on decorative knob which secured the end piece of the cotton when not in use; but on the whole they were more likely to allow the cotton to become unwound than the old cotton barrel. In some a small notch, similar to that found on our cotton reels today, has been made— probably by some inventive owner to overcome this difficulty.

By about 1830 the manufacturers were well on their way to making still cheaper and easier types of cotton reels. Largely because the advent of machinery made their large-scale and swift manufacture both possible and profitable, wooden reels made their appearance, and reels as we know them today were in to stay. However, at their inception they were not universally approved. They were not considered elegant enough to make their appearance, naked, in a lady's drawing-room and so some sort of covering had to be found for them. Thus we find sets of reel-holders coming into use, and a very charming innovation they were, being formed of a simple base and an ornamental top joined by a shank. The top was usually decorated with a formal or a floral design, and could either be unscrewed, or pulled off the shank by means of a small pin, and the cotton reel was then slipped on to the spindle and the top replaced. Some of these reel-holders are very charming indeed, being made in mother-of-pearl, or ivory, for the most part, though sometimes also in silver, or gold, or some other suitable material matching the other sewing implements in a fitted case. Usually they have a floral or a geometric design, or are shaped like a rose or daisy, or else they are intricately carved in ivory, and they form a most pleasing background to the coloured cottons and silks which they enclose.

Another item for which collectors should be on the look-out, but which are not easily come by, are the small boxes used to hold the fancifully wound cotton balls that came into fashion in the early nineteenth century. These are like small string-boxes with a hole in the lid or side, and are made in a variety of shapes and materials. Sometimes they are shaped like beehives, but more often are simply small circular boxes in ivory, tortoiseshell, mother-of-pearl or similar materials. Larger ones, usually in wood, bone, or ivory, were also used for wools. For winding clamps see page 140.

TAPE MEASURES

Amongst some of the smaller items found in needlework boxes are yard measures, or tape measures. The more correct name is actually yard measure, and they entered into history quite late in time. The old method of measuring was by the yardstick or meteyard, and most houses had such a stick handed down through generations as a treasured possession, since it was the only way of ensuring correct measurement, not only for materials, but in woodwork and other domestic matters. Very probably in about the 1600s, some inventive housewife thought of the bright idea of measuring off her own personal yard measure on to a piece of string, or tape, so that she might then carry it around with her in her pocket for convenience. The idea gradually spread, and eventually small boxes, with spindles on which the measure could be wound for neatness, were introduced: and so was born the tape measure as we know it today.

On the earliest tapes the only markings are long lines denoting the division of feet, and short lines denoting smaller measurements. It is only about the middle of the eighteenth century that we find neatly written figures beginning to divide the tape into inches, and even then many are still worked out in the old form of measurement, the 'nail' or 2¼in. This old form, however, is not often found after the beginning of the nineteenth century. At about this time, also, printed measures began to come into general use instead of the old hand-written ones.

These little yard measures offered scope for every shape and style of receptacle to be fashioned for their safe-keeping, and they have also been made in many combinations. Sometimes they are found with a needlecase or a pincushion or, very frequently, with thread-waxers. After use they had to be wound back again by the spindle handle—a very relaxing and soothing task missing from the use of our modern spring-type tape measures, where a slight pressure of the thumb makes the tape flash back into its case.

THREAD-WAXERS

Waxing is seldom used nowadays, except for certain types of embroidery and in specific trades such as cobbling, sailmaking and canvas work. But in earlier times it was used both to strengthen many types of threads, and also to enable them to slip more easily through the material. In days when nearly all garments had ruffles and gathers somewhere or other on them, this waxing was therefore an important, almost indispensible aid to sewing, and every workbox contained its cake of wax.

In the country, wax was often taken from the local hives, or from one's own personal hive, and then formed into plain little cakes, but in towns it was more usual to buy it in tiny cakes which were daintily wrapped and decorated with gold or silver papers. Sometimes such unused little wax cakes may still be found in needlework boxes, usually still in their gold or silver foil, and in a small box or wax container. But for actual use they were slipped into the special little thread-waxers which often formed part of the fittings of a box, and they were then easier and cleaner to handle.

These thread-waxers, though made in a variety of shapes, were basically composed of two discs which fitted over the top and bottom of the wax cake and were then pressed firmly in. Some were also in the form of a reel, with a central shank which passed through a hole in the wax. In the more elegantly fitted workboxes the thread-waxer usually matched the reel-holders for the silks and cottons, and they were frequently made of mother-of-pearl, carved ivory, horn or wood. Many were fitted on to a yard measure, or combined with an emery or pincushion. Once again, the variety of combinations achieved is wide enough to delight the hearts of all collectors.

The little cases in which the wax was kept prior to actual use are usually similar to thimble cases, and in the shape of fruit, acorns, small barrels or lanterns.

EMERIES

Linking up with all these small articles, and usually matching them in the fitted boxes, are emeries, frequently mistaken for pincushions.

These are small pads filled with fine emery powder and, in the days before stainless steel, they were essential for cleaning rust off needles. Before use, the needle was thrust into the emery pad and rubbed up and down several times until all the stains were removed and the blade was once more sharp and shining. They are normally smaller and heavier than pincushions, and a faint rasping sound may often be heard as the needle rubs against the emery powder, which is seldom heard in pincushions, even when stuffed with sawdust.

HAND-COOLERS

When we come to hand-coolers we enter the field of controversy. They are most commonly in the form of an egg, made of marble or other natural rocks or stones in plain or multi-colours, and they are supposed to have served the purpose of keeping the hands and fingers cool. This is essential to any embroideress, whose work may well be spoiled by hot, moist hands. The cool property of the marble was not easily impaired by over-warm fingers, and handling it was a daintier and more discreet way of keeping cool in public than the professional's use of powder or spirit, though these latter may be more effective over long, sustained periods of work.

Other eggs are made of earthenware or porcelain, and sometimes of wood, horn, etc. These are simply darning eggs. The china ones are often decorated with scenes, mottoes or texts, but they are usually distinguishable from the hand-cooler by their lighter weight, and also by the fact that, because of the material of which they are made, they do not possess the same quality of being bad conductors of heat as do the true hand-coolers, and thus they do not remain constantly cool.

Toilet waters were also frequently used, not only for their fragrance and as refreshment for headaches, but to keep hands cool and clean, and this explains why so many workboxes are fitted with scent flacons or bottles, and why, even when they are not actually fitments, they are frequently found amongst the contents of the boxes, or in the small purses which abound in most of them. Bristol blue glass, often gilded with the popular flower-and-bird ornament of the 1760s, or the later cut-Bristol types of the 1820s onwards, are frequent finds. Sometimes also, but more rarely, one comes upon the charming little Chelsea bottles in the form of small figures, usually of shepherds or shepherdesses, or peasant figures in a variety of poses.

VINAIGRETTES AND SMELLING-SALT BOTTLES

Vinaigrettes, too, often make their appearance in early nineteenty-century workboxes, and the specimen in the box featured on the cover of this book is a particularly lovely example, being of rock crystal and gold.

In this particular form, vinaigrettes have a short history of rather less than one hundred years' duration, but they spring from the old pouncet box and the pomander, and as late as the last years of the seventeenth century were known as sponge boxes, being used to keep the little pieces of sponge soaked in aromatic vinegars which our ancestors so often found not only useful, but necessary, in overcrowded, stuffy rooms and gatherings. Even at the beginning of the nineteenth century they were often known simply as aromatic vinegar cases or boxes. Because the acetic acid which forms the base of all these scented vinegars corrodes all metals save gold, the perforated grid through which the fragrance could be enjoyed had usually to be made of gold or some other metal coated with gold if the box was to endure. The container itself also usually had to be in either gold, glass, or a hard stone such as cornelian, agate, rock crystal, etc, or else lined to prevent contact between the casing and the potent acid.

Vinaigrettes come in a wide variety of shapes and forms: heart-shaped, round, or representing a walnut, strawberry or some other small fruit. But the majority tend to be rectangular for the simple reason that this places less wear and tear on the tiny double hinges necessary for opening the lid and the grid. These two coverings hinge on the same pin and thus the hinges and pin take a considerable amount of strain and have to be a perfect fit. The grilles through which the fragrance is inhaled are most beautifully pierced and engraved, often with tiny pictorial scenes or with elaborate scrollwork.

Vinaigrettes are found less and less frequently as the Victorian period draws on. The introduction of smelling salts in the middle years of the century marked the beginning of their decline. Small bottles gained the ascendancy once more and, towards the end of the century were frequently double-ended, a silver or gold cap at each end, one section being for scent, and the other for aromatic vinegar or smelling salts either in block or crystal form. Plain faceted glass, as well as red glass and the greenish glass popular with the Victorians was used, and such bottles are frequently found either fitted or loose, one popular form being the long, smooth type shown on page 144. Usually these have silver or gold stoppers with hallmarkings on them, and so can be dated with accuracy, and they were used in one or other form for scent or for smelling salts.

TRACING WHEELS

Another item sometimes found, but seldom fitted, unless it be in the compendium type of box, is a tool consisting of a long handle at the end of which is a small serrated, revolving wheel. This was used for marking out patterns on firm tissue or tracing paper, since the small teeth left little prick-marks behind them as the wheel was run carefully along the lines of the pattern. In late Victorian times it would more commonly have been used for marking out dress patterns or embroidery patterns, but once at least in its history it had had a different, and perhaps more interesting, purpose.

From the seventeenth century up to the early years of the nineteenth there had been a fashion for making 'pin-prickt pictures'. Some of these are extremely complicated and must have taken many hours to do, with figures and portraits all finely pricked out. Sometimes the central figure or the face and hands is painted in, but with borders in fine scrollwork and intricate geometrical designs being fully pricked. Many of these pictures, rare and valuable amongst collectors today, are of saints and popular martyrs, and were probably made by nuns in the various religious houses or by the young ladies of the great Roman Catholic families of England and the Continent.

Very briefly, the paper was placed upon a backing of some soft, but firm cloth, and then the main outline of the design was pricked with a pin on the right side. The paper was then lifted up and turned over on to the other side and the spaces in the leaves and flowers, or down the folds of garments, were filled in carefully with pin-pricks all placed very close together. The designs thus formed stood out very clearly and can be most intriguing and are usually most excellently executed. There is a diversity of opinion as to whether the designs were done all on the one side, or whether the paper was reversed and the pricking done in the manner described above; it is probable that both methods were used by different people, and certainly the way described would appear to have been the method used in those the writer has seen. In *An Old-fashioned Children's Book* by Andrew Tuer, the toothed wheel with sharp points just described is mentioned as being used for the outlines, though of course the filling process and small portions all had to be hand-pricked with a pin.

The mention of these pin-prickt pictures, and the sight of one of the small wheel-toothed markers which the writer possesses, brings to mind the tragic figure of Marie Antoinette. An attempt at her rescue was being devised by the Comte de Rougeville, and his plans to overpower her guards and take her to the Château de Livry where a large body of horsemen were waiting to conduct her into Austria and safety, were practically ready. The unhappy queen tried to send him a message from her prison, using a slip of thin paper, some 5in by 2in, on which she had painstakingly pricked out her message: *Je suis gardée à vue; je ne parle à personne. Je me fie à vous, je viendrai* (I see no one; I speak to no one. I trust myself to you, I shall come). But she was betrayed, and her pathetic little message was of no avail. Seven weeks later she was taken out to execution. It is said that she spent much of her time pin-pricking whilst in prison, even making out a list of her linen against the bare walls, since she had nothing else with which to occupy her hands or her mind. It would seem from this that pin-pricking was at that time a well-known occupation.

PENCILS AND NOTEBOOKS

Other items frequently met with in fitted cases are a pencil and sometimes a small notebook. These latter are similar to the little *carnets de bal* used by the ladies of the seventeenth and eighteenth centuries, and are normally of mother-of-pearl, ivory, silver or gold for the two covers, with several small pages of ivory for the sheets. On many of the little sheets, odd notes are still decipherable—reminders that a certain-coloured silk is running out or more waxes need to be purchased, or the prices of small items of expenditure, or the number of a pattern book. Two such small notebooks are illustrated on page 144.

Because rulers, pencils, pens and small ink-bottles are found iu Victorian boxes it does not always mean that these were a combined writing box and needlework box. Sometimes it is simply that such articles were necessary to the enthusiastic embroideress who wished to draw her own designs. A writing case is normally also fitted with pockets for the paper and letters, and will very often be in leather rather than in silk or velvet, and may have a small flat pad, sometimes with blotting-paper inserted, upon which the letters could be written.

LUCETS

Amongst some of the more strangely shaped objects to be found are small tools known as lucets (diagram, below). On the Continent this tool is sometimes called a hay-fork, which is a good descriptive name, especially when it is the type which has a long handle attached to it, which made for speedier working. These little gadgets were used for making cords, and for the most part they are to be found in plain or painted woods, horn and ivory. In the more fashionable circles, lucets were sometimes made in mother-of-pearl and tortoiseshell and, when a handle was attached, this would be very elegantly decorated. The cords made by this means were very strong and firm and, many people averred, infinitely superior to those which could be bought in the shops once machine-made cords became available in the late 1700s. To be able to make one's own cord on the lucet had, moreover, the

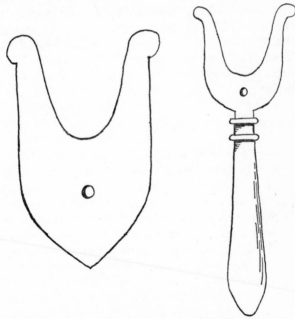

17   *Lucet, approx 4in high; and a lucet with handle, approx 9in*

added advantage of enabling the colours of both cord and fabric to be matched perfectly, since the same silks or yarns could be used on both, or even threads of the material itself could be used. However, as with so much else, home cordmaking was gradually superseded by the machine-made varieties, and lucets fell out of use. They had a brief return during the mid-nineteenth century, and a slightly half-hearted début in the Edwardian era, but they never really caught on again. Nevertheless, they usually remained in the workboxes where they had lain for so long, and are still frequently to be found in them today.

WOOL AND SILK HOLDERS

Wool and silk holders come in a variety of forms, but an especially pleasing style is that of a beehive, frequently in turned and polished rosewood for wools, and in ivory for smaller balls of silk. Usually the base unscrews, and there is a hole at the side and sometimes through the top for the thread to be drawn through. Many also have a spindle which fitted on to the winder used whilst the ball was being wound up from the original skein or shank. These are larger than the boxes mentioned on page 130, and the hole for the spindle, or the spindle itself, usually denotes the difference.

MAGNIFYING GLASSES

Other aids to fine needlework to be found are magnifying glasses or lenses, sometimes with a handle, or sometimes on a small stand. Occasionally folding ones may be found. The latter are usually in brass or other metal with an opening, which usually measures 1in square, in the bottom piece of the metal. These were used for counting linen threads. Some also have double lenses, and can be clamped on to the edge of a frame, and these were an aid to working and to examining the finer types of embroidery to check on accuracy.

CLAMPS

Sometimes an object is found in an old box which looks very

much like a workbench vice. It may well be in steel, or in wood, and may seem a little out of place amongst needlework tools. Upon closer examination such an article will normally prove to be a needlework clamp of one or other of the various types known to us. The main purpose of this item was to clamp the material to the table in order to keep the work firm for sewing. This meant that a long piece of hemming then needed only one hand to hold it taut, leaving the other free for the stitching. In the days before the sewing machine, every seam and every hem for the whole household had to be done by hand, including not only clothing, but bedlinen, tablecloths, wall hangings and other domestic articles. Thus the clamp was an important piece of equipment and made the needlewoman's task far quicker and less laborious. Quite often a pincushion is found fitted to the top of a clamp, and this served not only as a depository for spare pins, but also enabled the more delicate fabrics to be pinned securely to the velvet of the pincushion rather than placed under the clamp itself.

Most of the early examples of clamps, from the late 1700s to early 1800s, likely to come into the hands of collectors today are of polished and turned woods. Later ones are frequently of steel, often cut and faceted and very decorative in their own fashion, and some of these also are still to be found. In late-Victorian times sewing clamps gradually became plainer and heavier in construction, perhaps because they were no longer so necessary to the ordinary needlewoman now that the sewing machine had come to stay. Often they will have a print glued and varnished on to their wooden surfaces, the pictures frequently being of the memento variety denoting some seaside or other resort. The Victorians were great enthusiasts for holidays and travel.

Clamps were made in a wide variety of shapes and forms, according to the use to which they would be put, and most of the later ones are too large to have a place within a workbox. Nevertheless, for recognition purposes, a brief mention of the various types may not be out of place.

Some hemming clamps have a small spindle and reel attached, and just in front of the reel there is a small knob. These are a combination of sewing and netting clamps, and it is the small knob which indicates the specific purpose. Quite often they are in ivory, and when actually fitted in a needlework box they, together with the netting needles, shuttles and gauges, are frequently elaborately carved to match the other implements.

Separate from the sewing clamp is the winding clamp. Smaller versions of this may still be found in worktables. The more elaborate ones are sometimes of ivory or horn, but the types most frequently met with are of polished wood, and have a spindle and a winding frame, or cradle, above the actual clamp itself. There is an especially beautiful specimen of a wool-winder and clamp combined, made of whalebone, in the Hull Museum, but on the whole most of them were of simpler construction. They were used for winding silks, cottons or wools, all of which, until the early nineteenth century, were bought in skeins or hanks but then had to be wound by hand on to reels, holders or winders (see page 127) before they could be used. With these later winding clamps, one person could wind unaided by another holding the skein or hank to prevent it becoming tangled.

Winding clamps were used in pairs, unlike the much larger, four-pegged, single knitting-winder still in use today. The skein was stretched between the two winders, and so allowed the thread to run freely. In the larger versions, the cradle may be from 4 to 6in high, which enabled them to be used for wool-winding, but the types used for silks are smaller, the cradles sometimes being merely an inch or two in height. In many, as already mentioned, the spindle terminates in a knob. This was used for anchoring the loop when netting work was in progress. Others have a small cup in which the ball of wool could rest when the winding was unfinished or had to be temporarily laid aside. Clamps are, incidentally, an excellent example of a tool which has evolved through the years into the most convenient and practical form. Time and motion study was not discovered in our day!

Special mention must be made of a form of clamp known as the hemming bird, which today is all too often only found in museums. Nevertheless, a keen collector would not wish to fail to recognise one if he or she had the very good fortune to come across such an item. They are more likely to be found in the USA rather than in England or on the Continent, since they were extremely popular there in the early days of the last century. They were originally made in Georgian days, probably more in the nature of novelties or 'toys', and the metal bird surmounting the clamp opens and closes its beak as the tail is depressed or released. Thus the bird's beak itself formed the actual clamp, and the material was inserted there. In very many ways it was an improvement on the more ordinary type of clamp, since mere pressure of the hand could be used to change the position of the work, without having to loosen the screw underneath the table.

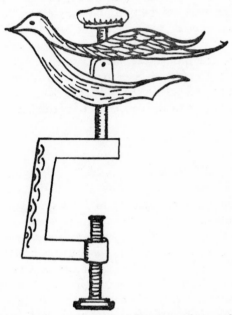

18   *Steel hemming bird c 1800, used for holding materials firm while hemming*

In the United States these hemming birds or sewing birds were also often called 'grippers', which is an apt, though clearly less elegant, description of their purpose. They were frequently made by the local blacksmith or a cutler, and so vary considerably in style and in accessories which accompanied them. Gradually butterflies and animal forms appeared in place of the original bird, but these were never quite so popular. In America, in particular, the hook found with many was used for rug-making, and such clamps are still sometimes called rug-braiders today. Quite often, also, these sewing birds had pincushions added on to their backs or fitted on to a slender support above them.

There is an interesting hemming bird in the State Historical Museum in Moscow. It is in metal, fairly plain, but is a charming example of a Continental style of the early 1800s. In the London Museum there are some interesting specimens of the more fanciful forms of sewing clamps which eventually evolved from the simple bird type. They are made of cast metal, and are surmounted by slightly ornate figures of dolphins, cherubs and other fancies.

Like so many other tools, with the sewing machine striding firmly on in the steps of progress, these 'toys' and joys of the needlewoman fell into disuse, and today many people would be hard put to it to give any explanation of a hemming bird's use if they were to find one. They are a relic of the past, but a most interesting addition to any collection of needlework tools.

PENKNIVES FOR PARFILAGE

A penknife, or folding-knife, is often included in the simplest of needlework boxes, and we should recall that these tools were used not only for sharpening the nib of a quill pen, but also for quite a number of small needlework tasks. Such knives probably developed side by side with, if not from, the old seam-knife used for unpicking seams and often for cutting buttonholes or for manipulating small cuts and snips where scissors might be less reliable to handle. Penknives found in earlier workboxes bring back a memory of a craze which flourished at the court of Louis XVI, and which eventually found its way over half the Continent of Europe and even across the Channel, where it was in vogue for some fifty years or so. This was the practice of parfilage, or 'drizzling', and necessitated the use of a stiletto, or finely pointed instrument, a pair of scissors and a penknife. It consisted of unpicking and unravelling all the gold and silver trimmings which the extravagances of fashion dictated on the outer garments of the day. Gold and silver thread are extremely costly, since they do in fact consist of real gold and real silver wrapped round an inner core of silk; the gold laces and rich gold trimmings of the day

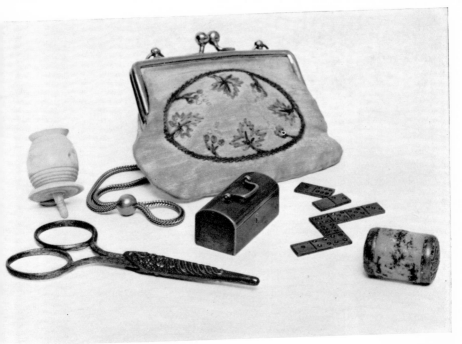

Page 143 (above) Mid-Victorian purse with silver mount; ivory cotton barrel without handle; miniature metal chest with metal dominoes, Victorian scissors in metal sheath and thread-waxer with wax in place; (below) top left, retractable crochet hook, agate hand cooler, ivory stiletto, shuttle, early Victorian stork scissors, ivory silk-holder and spindle, screw-top cotton barrel, silver tatting shuttle, ivory and ebony book needlecase, ivory needlecase in form of a peapod, probably c 1800. In centre, mother-of-pearl box containing thread-winders

Page 144 (right) *Leather pin-cushion with raffia embroidery, c 1840. Victorian double-ended wooden needleholder; needlecase with polished satinwood covers and pictorial scene. Below, a typical beadwork purse with ivory mount, c 1850 and an early-Victorian needlecase in patchwork decorated with beadwork and with pinsticking round edge; (below) Victorian silver bag mount decorated with engraving, mother-of-pearl and cabochon bloodstones. Below a small ivory stiletto between two mid-Victorian scent bottles, with silver stoppers, with another similar below. On right, 19th-century ivory crochet hook, two small notebooks with ivory and mother-of-pearl covers and ivory pages and a 19th-century mother-of-pearl crochet hook* were therefore extremely valuable, and it became not only fashionable, but almost a virtue, to spend spare moments in unpicking the gold and silver threads of laces, froggings, braids and other decorations from disused garments. Once unpicked, the threads were returned to the lacemen, or other tradesmen by whom such items were supplied, who then made allowance against the value, or else were actually prepared to buy them back. Eventually they were sold back to the goldsmith, who melted them down and thus was left with the pure metal from which he could begin anew. It was a virtue so closely allied to greed as to become in time almost indistinguishable.

Ladies of fashion were, naturally, foremost in the taste for this craze, partly because they alone were likely to wear clothing decorated so extravagantly, and also because it helped cut down the full cost of their own clothing. It was, in fact, a very valuable form of pin-money. And since it was a fashionable craze, it demanded fashionable implements with which to practise it. Large embroidered bags were carried, in which the unpicked gold and silver thread could be placed when ready, and the three essential small implements were often found together in a small pochette, or sometimes in special 'drizzling sets'. The craze never caught on so extensively in England as on the Continent, though in the early years of the nineteenth century it had its ardent devotees even amongst members of the royal household. Here in England, however, it was for the most part a domestic pastime, practised in the privacy of the home, though it was permissible to do it there amongst company, since it was a harmless enough occupation for the hands and regarded as a most praiseworthy and thrifty task. For this reason few parfilage sets seem to have been introduced into England on the whole, but the familiar long-pointed steel stiletto, scissors and penknife, found in many fitted cases of the era, bear witness to the fact that it was not an unknown practice even here.

CHAPTER 9

OTHER ITEMS

Workboxes really ought to be called the 'collector's joy'. Quite apart from their own appeal and that of their more legitimate fittings, they have the added attraction that one never knows what is going to be discovered till one begins rummaging. Each may be a veritable museum in miniature, with its own range of fascinating objects, each of which can lead to further exploration and research.

At least one item seems to be common to all types of workboxes, whether they be the elegant worktables of the late eighteenth century, the simpler workboxes of the Victorian era, or the ordinary wickerwork basket which replaced them—nearly every one contains a greater or lesser miscellany of buttons. For those who have previously been misguided enough to imagine that a button is merely an object of personal utilitarian or ornamental use in sartorial fields, it may come as a surprise to know that the United States has a National Button Society which issues a bi-monthly *National Button Bulletin* for the benefit of the many thousands of ardent collectors in this field. A button there may change hands for more than $100, and many fetch $12 to $50 on the open market. There is nothing mean about American collectors: those who want an item and know that it is of genuine value are prepared to pay its catalogue price without haggling, or to bid at auction in a fair open market. As with everything else North Americans tackle, button collectors have brought to their task a boundless enthusiasm and thoroughgoing attention to detail. Besides magazines on the subject, an efficient organisation of 'button clubs' is run on similar lines to the postal-stamp clubs known to philatelists in England. There are even mail-order auctions of buttons, and competitive exhibitions arranged by the various State button societies and similar groups; there are also a number of museums which have comprehensive collections of historic buttons.

In England button collecting appears to be on a more restricted scale as yet, having been largely confined to service and uniform buttons, or to the very beautiful, but much more rare, jewel and paste buttons of the pre-Revolution days of France. There is therefore scope for the beginner to enter a relatively untapped market in which his greatest asset may prove to be the number of acquaintances he can muster who have the 'junk' of several generations still stored away in attics, old boxes and suitcases, or in drawers where discarded clothes and button boxes may still bring to light treasures untold.

So far as their history goes, buttons cannot really claim a notable lineage before the early Middle Ages. M. D. C. Crawford, in *The Influence of Invention on Civilization*, credits Paleolithic man with the invention of the toggle and possibly the button, and this latter may be true, but many experts dispute it. The clothing of the ancient Western civilisations did not call for buttoning, since it consisted mainly of flowing garments secured by clasps, girdles, or buckles. It is not until the elegant, more tailored types of Persian clothing were introduced into Europe that the history of buttons proper may be said to begin so far as this Continent is concerned. It was the invasions of the Mohammedans in the seventh century which introduced Persian styles of dress to some extent, and the Crusaders are believed to have spread the fashion further, but it is doubtful whether the Persians actually invented buttons themselves. It may well be that they had their true origin in China.

From old French documents many interesting facts may be gleaned about these small objects. We learn that François I in the sixteenth century ordered of 'Jacques Polin, goldsmith, living on Le Pont-au-Change, 13,600 gold buttons' which were to be used to decorate a robe of black velvet. Enamel buttons were also popular, and in the next century the cost of buttons used by the extravagant Louis XIV (1643–1715) must have been a considerable drain on the finances of the Treasury. A number of items from the *Register des Pierreries et Presents du Roy*, which was kept by the minister of foreign affairs, indicate just how fully the king satisfied his personal taste for luxury:

3 Feb 1685   24 diamond buttons, worth 138,030 livres.

7 March 1685   made and delivered by the Sieur Bose, six diamond buttons —30,000 livres.

26 July 1685   delivered by Montarsy to the Marquis de Seigueley for the King, 75 diamond buttons—587,703 livres.

26 July 1685   Montarsy provided 48 gold buttons, each enriched by a diamond and 96 buttonmakers gave 48 buttons made up of 5 diamonds each and 48 of a single stone each, for the King's dress—for 185,123 livres.

And when they said 'diamonds' they meant exactly that. The hard, brilliant form of glass we know as paste, or strasse, was not discovered and perfected by Joseph Strassen until the middle of the eighteenth century.

Unfortunately, very few of the really valuable buttons made of precious stones have survived from this era, and collectors' pieces are difficult to come by and extremely expensive. Simply because they were so valuable, and because it was comparatively easy to prise out the stones and melt down the metal when a financial crisis was on hand, not many of these buttons found their way into family workboxes; they were instead translated into hard cash for the family coffers. Even eighteenth-century paste buttons always had a market value and are therefore not frequently found. But buttons dating from the early nineteenth century onwards still abound. There are beautiful specimens among these, in enamels, china, metal, glass, and a wide variety of other materials, and this is a field where collectors really stand a chance of finding exciting varieties. A forthcoming book by Miss Primrose Peacock, from which I have been privileged to glean some information, will be essential for any would-be collector, as it will give excellent photographs of hundreds of examples of very beautiful and unusual buttons of the nineteenth century, together with full descriptions to enable a collector to recognise the various types.

After buttons, the most usual items found in old workboxes are often buckles and clasps. They come in all shapes and sizes. Their history dates back to the earliest days of civilisation, and buckles in a variety of shapes and forms, utilitarian and ornamental, have come down to us from Greek and Roman times, whilst Celtic art produced some of the finest and most beautiful forms known to us.

Unfortunately collectors are very unlikely to come across any of the lovely seventeenth- and eighteenth-century buckles which so delighted the courtesans and the *beaux* of those days—which is a pity, since quite apart from the beautiful pastes of the later part of the era, there are specimens of cut and faceted steel, of finely wrought and chased silver and other metals, and others decorated with fine enamels and porcelain plaques, which makes the collecting of these items a sheer delight. H. R. D'Allemagne deals at length with these in his book, and illustrates the chapter lavishly with rare and exceptional specimens.

But nevertheless we are quite likely to find examples of the dress, shoe, hat, and belt buckles and clasps of the nineteenth century, which have an interest of their own and are still a relatively untapped field for collectors. Some will be in imitation paste, some in steel or silver, finely engraved or chased. Pairs of shoe buckles are quite common, as also are belt buckles and clasps. Two very interesting examples of the latter were seen recently in the bottom of an old box, and were mid-nineteenth century, made of silver, and some 7in combined length. One pair formed the outspread, batlike wings of a devil, the grinning, horned head forming the actual fastening, whilst the other was in the form of an eagle, the feathers of the outstretched wings beautifully worked in detail, and the head, slightly turned to one side, again forming the clasp.

Belt clasps are also found in the form of clasped hands, but perhaps the most usual 'finds' are the rounded or rectangular forms, either as clasps or as buckles. These are often adorned with all manner of pictorial scenes, with cupids and with floral swags and luscious-looking fruits. Buckles and clasps were worn on shoes, hats, skirts, and with dresses, right up to Edwardian times, so plenty remain for the collector to expend his time and energy on their gradual accumulation.

But amongst some of the most interesting articles to be found in old workboxes are those which, by their intensely personal nature, open to us a vista of the lives and history of former days—little yellowed scraps of paper with fading writing, little messages speaking across the years to any who will listen and try to understand the words behind the words.

One especially moving little reminder of history was in the box mentioned in Chapter 1, made by an American Indian woman for her beloved mistress, Peggy Arnold, wife of the notorious General Benedict Arnold. On the flyleaf of the birchbark needlecase, in faded ink, and in her own handwriting, is the message Elasaba sent with her gift, a simple verse, little more than doggerel, but speaking a wealth of love and loyal devotion.

> When more pleasing scenes engage
> And you in polished circles shine,
> Then let this wild, savage page
> Declare that gratitude is mine.

October 7th 1791   Elasaba of the Micmac tribe

It brings vividly to the mind's eye the rather sad story of Peggy Shippen, the darling of Philadelphian society, and often called 'the most fascinating woman in America'. Whilst the British Army was occupying Philadelphia she became very friendly with Major John Andre but later, upon the British withdrawal, married Benedict Arnold, then a rising military man. At the time in the War of Independence when things were not going well for the Americans, General Arnold was in charge of West Point, and negotiated secretly for the sale of its military defences with the British. Major Andre, as a former friend of the family, and as one who knew Philadelphia well, was detailed to go to the general's house to work out the final arrangements for the deal. Unfortunately, he was recognised whilst leaving the house and captured. Since he was wearing civilian dress rather than military uniform, he was treated as a spy and hanged instead of being shot, and this caused a tremendous wave of indignation in both England and America. General Arnold was disgraced, and had to flee to England, and today in the USA his name is still synonymous with treachery. Some time later he and his wife spent several years in New Brunswick and the West Indies, and it was in New Brunswick, in 1791, on their departure for England again, that Elasaba made this beautiful box for her mistress.

In a secret drawer below the taller of the two wooden boxes

shown on page 90 was a small piece of paper which said: 'Jane's box just as she left it.' On the back was another message: 'Eliza's sister—died young. Favourite brother died at sea', and, rather pathetically, in amongst the silks also contained in the drawer I found a pendant brass anchor with rope twining round the shaft and a little scrap of paper with the date '1838'.

A typically Victorian mode of thought is expressed on paper in an Indian carved box, headed: 'From Maria Russell's diary. 20 Marina, St. Leonards, 18th and 19th, 1854.' The extract goes on:

18th. Uncle William came down. He brought down a little tin box from the Indian box. What can it be? I hope it is something for Frances . . .

19th. Uncle William opened the tin box and there was a beautiful work-box carved in sandalwood. It was for me. How very kind of Uncle Henry to send it to me when there were so many people to send it to! I think it is the most beautiful thing I have seen. It is perfectly lovely in all its parts. It is incomparable! Its beauty is inexpressible. It is a chef d'oeuvre . . .

Though we shall never know which month it was that Uncle William actually visited St Leonards and gave the sandalwood box to Maria Russell, the tenor of her thoughts is communicated to us, fresh and vigorous after nearly 120 years. One wonders who Frances was, and whether she was as generously minded as Maria and rejoiced that the box with its 'incomparable' and 'inexpressible' beauty was given to another.

In another box I came across a twist of faded tissue which enclosed a pinpaper of the tiniest possible pins, of the type usually called 'Lilliputian', together with a lock of hair. The little accompanying note reads: 'These pins were used for dressing my darling when a baby. 1834' and 'my darling's hair when fourteen months old'. They conjure up the vision of some mother of long ago attending to her baby's toilet with careful love; but what garments did she entrust to those tiny pins, and did babies squirm less then than now, that she dared use such small, sharp implements?

In yet another box, a note enclosed with a fairly large square of heavy brocaded material in a deep wine-red with dark green and blue flowers on it gave, surprisingly, the information that, 'This was great grandmama's wedding dress, on the occasion of her marriage in May, 1781.' Then, sadly, the story was finalised for us: 'She died in Oct. 1783 whilst on holiday in Ireland.' Who was the nameless great grandmama; was she perhaps a widow that her dress was not the usual bridal white, and why did she die so soon and so unexpectedly in the midst of that Irish holiday? We shall never know, but somewhere, all those years ago, the wedding dress was laid carefully away long, long before her descendants cut from it the scrap of material and noted down so carefully the brief outlines of her married life. We need to touch these treasures of long ago with gentle hands and gentler minds, for they were all part of the life-blood of men and women of long ago!

And what Nanny was it wrote inside the cover of an old, finely worked cross-stitched needlecase: 'Master Jamie's first piece of work. Given to his dear Mama on her birthday, Aug. 19, 1797'? Master Jamie's 'first piece of work', so carefully dated and recorded, is about 3in long by 1¾in deep, and consists of the alphabet, the numerals from 1 to 9, and the pious hope 'May God bless us all', together with the initials JM and the surprising information 'aged seven'. I have come across many instances of this very fine cross and tent stitching worked on tiny samplers and needlecases by small boys, indicating that it was not only the little girls who had to sit still for long hours assiduously working away at their embroideries.

And why did I find that white fan with its pierced ivory sticks wrapped up and laid away so carefully in the secret drawer of an old workbox, with a little note written in fine, elegant script: 'Jenny's fan for her first ball. 1843'? Why was Jenny's fan so carefully kept and hidden away? Did she use it for that first ball, and never again, or did she never go to the ball? No one can tell us now, but how much such little things highlight for us the ways and lives of other days.

Not all scraps of paper found in old workboxes are so sentimental. Sometimes there are wrapping papers still containing part of their original contents and giving a taste of early Victorian sales promotion methods. One such, on very fine tissue paper, had a drawing of a Japanese lady engagingly swirling a fan, and read as follows:

LIBERTY AND CO
East India Merchants of 218 Regent Street
Write for Illustrated Catalogue (forwarded post free)

After a list of the various art forms and treasures available there is a happy reminder of days now far off: 'Prices from 1/– to £500'!

Frequently also, as he rummages through, the inquiring collector will find small leather wallets about 1½in high, which contain *Tilt's Miniature Almanack*. These tiny almanacs were issued yearly and contained, in addition to a diary, a wealth of informative details which make *Moore's Almanack* seem almost insignificant. They date back from 1890 or so; 1834 is the earliest I have so far found.

During the nineteenth century there was a craze for miniature games, which were carried in ladies' pockets or bags, or in their workboxes, where so many are still to be found. Horn or ivory eggs, with fine beadwork covers, are firm favourites and usually hold tiny dominoes less than ½in long. Sometimes they hold small dice, sometimes counters. Chinese games were also much in vogue, and beautifully engraved mother-of-pearl playing pieces in the shape of fish are frequently encountered. Charms and typical Victorian mementoes are also frequent finds—little boots, or tiny inch-long books with peepshows in them revealing 'A View of Felixstowe' or some other favourite resort, or miniature *Bibles* and *The Life of our Lord* in pictures so small that a magnifying glass is needed to view them.

In one box was found a small gold filigree representation of a hand with three fingers and two thumbs. Clearly it was a charm of some sort, but it came as a surprise when the owner of the box told me that it was known as 'The Hand of Fatima' and was a favourite form of charm a century ago. Fatima, Mohammed's wife, is reputed to have had this particular deformity. Beyond the more ordinary types of charms often found on bracelets, I have also found in an old box a lion's tooth, a tiger's claw mounted with a silver ring for suspension, the famous 'monkey's paw' talisman, and very often the three monkeys who 'hear no evil, see no evil, and think no evil'.

Buttonhooks are frequently found in workboxes and were

probably there not so much as a toilet article (which would most likely have been kept elsewhere), but simply in order that when buttonholes were being made, they could be tested quickly and easily for size with the actual button to be used. The Victorians seldom used their fingers for a task when there was any implement available for the purpose.

Many boxes also have miniature whisks or brushes for keeping the small compartments clean. They are made in dozens of shapes and materials. One of the most charming recently met with was of olive-green ribbon and silver thread. The handle was formed of the ribbon wound round a hard core of firm stuffing, and the brush was composed of half a dozen loose pieces of the ribbon. Experiment proved it to be highly effective, since at the handle tip there was also a small, stiffish wire 'whisk' formed of short pieces of the wiry silver thread which reached into the most difficult corners of the little velvet-lined compartments.

During Victoria's reign there was a vogue for stamped paperwork and many cards, as well as envelopes opening out to disclose a picture or a message inside, may still be found, their sentiments obviously treasured for many years. This type of paperwork is similar to the stamped paper doyleys which are bought today in openwork floral and geometrical designs. The envelopes usually have a greater or lesser amount of this type of decoration on their four folding flaps which, when opened out, reveals a printed message, usually surrounded by coloured flower sprays, on the envelope's inner side. One, recently seen, would rejoice the hearts of mail service sales managers today. Instead of the gentle pressure of the, 'Someone, somewhere, is waiting for a letter from you . . .' type of reminder, these Victorian ones took the attack directly into the enemy's camp, for example:

> You Owe Me a Letter!
> Don't say 'I don't know
> What it is that I owe'
> Than you few have memory better.
> So I beg you will pay
> Without further delay,
> You know that you owe me—a Letter!

Puzzles, too, were greatly beloved by the Victorians, and

the following is a typical example of one in stamped paper-work:

```
P  A  O  U  A  T  Y  O
U  N  Y  S  H  I  O  U
K  D  D  H  T  L  D  L
O  D  N  A  E  O  U  O
O  O  A  L  E  V  O  V
L  W  N  L  S  E  Y  E
            ME?
```

The answer is given by reading up and down the columns be-ginning at the lower left-hand corner: 'Look up and down and you shall see that I love you Do you love me?'

In one box, the owner still keeps her grandfather's proposal to his wife, which had been kept tucked away safely in the top flap of the box for more than half a century. It is a large paperwork double-card, with a great deal of ornament and with padded lilies of the valley, roses, and forget-me-nots. In bold, clear writing, though faded by the passage of time, the proposal conveys its message in homemade poetry:

> Timorous when near, tho' bold when far away,
> I fain before you my petition lay.
> Doubt not, I love you more at every meeting.
> I ask you to be mine, as time is fleeting.
> Oh say those words, all other words above,
> 'I will be yours', then you the best I love.

Birthday and anniversary greetings abound in these paperwork cards—verses to 'Mother dear . . .' to rejoice any Victorian mama's heart with their devotion, 'Happy be thy birthday' and 'May this wedding day be blest' and others of a similar nature. One seen long ago and clearly the painstaking work of a young child was unfortunate in its expression, having an uncorrected spelling mistake in amongst the gaily coloured flowers and cut-work: 'Happy be Thy Weeding Day'. . . !

A message which seems particularly typical of the sentiment of the period was in two verses and was clearly a card of greetings for a birthday—very possibly for a twenty-first birthday. Too long to quote in full here, the first verse bade the recipient look around at all the blessings he had enjoyed in life, to remember all the gifts, joys, talents, love and friendship he had received and then, with a heart full of boundless gratitude, to say, 'Happy was my natal day!' The second verse exhorted him so to order his days and character that all who came into contact with him would regard it as a joy and privilege, and ever be able to say, 'Happy was thy natal day!'

A sadder keepsake was a mourning card with cut-out angels and a deep mourning band edging it all round, which said:

> England's Affectionate Token of Remembrance
> of His Royal Highness Prince Albert,
> The Beloved Husband of Her Most Gracious
> Majesty, Queen Victoria, Who Departed
> this life at Windsor Castle, on
> Saturday, Dec. 14th, 1861, at 10.50 p.m.
> in the 43rd year of his age.

Another such, perhaps even more poignant, merely had a thin black line around it with a border of daisies and lilies of the valley and the words:

> Little one, though short thy stay
> Every hour of it was gay;
> May such memories remain
> Cancelling out the grief and pain.

With the industry native to their generation, the ladies of the mid and late Victorian periods kept their friends, relatives and acquaintances supplied with a copious stream of embroidered texts, greetings, and noble thoughts. These were frequently worked on cards which were covered with small perforations, similar, in miniature, to the pegboard of today. The embroideress then worked a border round the card in a variety of stitches and colours, using the perforated holes as ready-made needle insertions, and then worked her verse or design in the centre in the same manner. It was a quick way of ensuring neatness and accuracy of stitchery, though doubtless the true embroideress looked upon such methods with scorn and thought they were a form of cheating. These little cards seem to have been bought in packets, many of which still remain in the lower sections of old caskets, and the variety of sentiments found in them seems to be endless. Sometimes the pattern was already printed on, and sometimes it was left to the ingenuity of the owner to design her own. They were used as greeting cards, bookmarkers, needlecase covers, small plaques to be hung on the walls or merely as gifts to be given when visiting, or to callers. Their sentiments include such things as the ever-popular 'God bless you', 'Health and Happiness to the Bride and Groom', 'No †, No 👑', *'Keine ohne Dornen'* (Nothing without thorns), *'Denk an mir'* (Think of me), 'May this House be Blessed', 'All Happiness be Thine' and similar tokens of regard. They are interesting as examples of the importance that Victorians placed on anniversaries and occasions of all kinds, since so many refer to birthdays, weddings, births, deaths and 'travelling mercies' besought; and also as indications of the close-knit community relationships they knew.

There was no problem then of 'Who am I?' Everyone had a place, and everyone had a duty to those above, around, and below him in society. The very fact of involvement in that duty made for stability, and little tokens constantly given and received kept the individual very much aware of his involvement. With cards on walls, in drawers, in boxes or on personal possessions, all stating either the recipient's or the donor's name, it must indeed have been difficult to lose consciousness of identity—'From your Aunt Jane', 'To my dearest second cousin, Annie', 'To Annie from her cousin Jack', 'To Annie from her Great Aunts Rebecca and Lavinia', 'To my granddaughter from Grandma Hetherington', 'To Annie from her Godmother, Frances G. Alton' and so on. Judging from the evidence of the constant flow of small gifts and tokens of regard and remembrance found in our search through old workboxes and coffers, it might well be true to say of these long-dead Victorians, 'Lo, how they loved one another', at least within their own circle of friends and relations, even though the modern generation scoffs at them as hypocritical.

CHAPTER 10

HOW TO BEGIN A COLLECTION

A would-be collector may well ask, 'How do I begin to collect needlework boxes, or the various accessories associated with them? How much should I pay for various items? How do I learn to know the true from the false?' To answer such questions is a very large order, but this chapter will provide a brief summing up of the subject; some guides to the dating of workboxes were mentioned in Chapter 1.

First and foremost, this is one of the safer fields for small collectors, simply because individual items are seldom so highly priced as to make it worth the while for unscrupulous dealers to start faking them. An object has to be in itself of very considerable value, or else widely sought after, to make it a paying proposition for anyone to go to the trouble and expense of making fake copies.

Let it be said at once that really fine old boxes, in absolutely first-class condition, dating from 1750–80 or so, are comparatively rare and difficult to find. They can probably only be bought today by private treaty, or through really reputable antique dealers and auctioneers. Such boxes can be worth considerable sums, depending entirely on the intrinsic value of their various fittings. A really fine rosewood box, with lining in good condition, and with fittings of gold and mother-of-pearl, dating from the late eighteenth century, might well come into the price range of £200–£300, or $500 to $800 in the United States, depending entirely upon the quality of the box as a whole. A nineteenth-century box, however, in really fine condition and with similar fittings to the one just mentioned, might well need to be insured for £150, or $300–400; a similar one with plain mother-of-pearl fittings might sell for as little as £20 or £30, or a mere $50–70. Equally, it could be picked up for between £2 ($4.80) and £5 ($12) at a local auction if it was the collector's lucky day. The differences in price depend on the general conditions of the box, its age and the materials used, counterbalanced by one other all-important factor, namely, how many people are interested in that particular item at that particular moment of sale.

With certain boxes, other factors as well would influence price. For instance, as yet I have never been fortunate enough to see a box entirely made and fitted by Carl Fabergé, but if such a box is in existence, in perfect condition, with no fittings missing, and if it is undoubtably genuine, signed and executed at the peak of his career, then it might well reach £1,000 ($2,400) or more at auction. It would be Fabergé's name which was the real selling point, whereas a box by an unnamed workman using the very same materials and styles might fetch only half the price. In the world of art and antiques it is not true to say that a rose by any other name would smell as sweet.

Another factor which increases value is whether an item has documentary evidence to prove that it has some particular association with history or with a historic personality. Thus, if a box were one day to come to light which had once belonged to Marie Antoinette, for instance, and *if it had documentary proof supporting the claim*, as contrasted with hearsay and belief, then such a box too might well fetch four figures. Unsupported by such evidence it would simply sell for its period value. But it must be said at once that the chance of such a find is minimal, and this is merely offered as an example of the difference which documentary evidence has upon value when any item is at sale.

To sum up, every collector ought to bear in mind that the value of any article, be it a water-melon or a Louis XV chair, is related to three basic factors. The first is the intrinsic value of the object itself; that is to say, the material of which it is made within the limitations of its range and type, and whether it has an inherent value due to rarity, age, or historical association, etc. The second is the sentimental value. This is difficult to assess. It will make an object worth £1,000 to a certain person or a group of persons, whilst to others it will be almost worthless. It will represent the desire the individual has for that particular object, perhaps because it will complete some other set, or perhaps because it may remind him of something or someone way back in his youth. It is the sort of thing unscrupulous dealers play upon when once they recognise it in a prospective purchaser. The third factor is that all value fluctuates and depends basically upon the law of supply and demand, on how many people want any particular item, or whether no one at all is interested in it. This is the sort of factor which takes over in times of war, famine, or other disasters, and which turns ordinary ideas of value upside down. Face to face with death by starvation for himself and his family, a man might well part with a Picasso for a bushel of wheat.

Thus value is relative, and probably in no area is it more important to remember this than when collecting items which are either comparatively plentiful or, as yet, not widely sought after. And by 'comparatively plentiful' is meant that, given time and careful searching in the right places, it is reasonable to expect that a given item will eventually be obtainable, but not necessarily that they abound in every good antique shop along select thoroughfares, nor in every second-hand or junk store down promising little by-ways.

One example which may serve to illustrate this point concerns the collecting of Victorian silver thimbles, particularly those from mid and late Victorian times. These were made, literally in their thousands, at a time when silver was probably cheaper and more plentiful than at any other time in modern history. Whilst not exactly 'two a penny', this phrase certainly describes their quantitative value, and they are, in fact, not usually worth more, intrinsically, than 15p. Broadly speaking, the average Victorian silver thimble, undecorated by precious stones or anything of that nature, and dating from about 1850 onwards, is almost worthless. Obviously there are exceptions, but these examples will be so very different from the usual run of Victorian thimble as to be immediately recognisable. In my search for old thimbles, dealers have often given me the scrap-box in which they put all small pieces of silver, broken chains and so on for sale as scrap metal eventually, to let me sort through it. If eventually I find a thimble it is almost certain to be one of the type described. Apart from research work (when all sorts of specimens are useful to have on hand for purposes of comparison) they are really of no particular value and most dealers, knowing this full well, will simply ask 10p or so, or a few cents, as being what they might expect to get for its scrap-metal value. Even remembering the present increasing rise in silver value, one has to offset this by the very small, almost negligible weight of silver in these old thimbles. But just occasionally I have come across a similar example in a shop window, or whilst browsing round the interior, and have been asked £1·25 ($3) for it, or slightly more, whereupon I have put it down firmly and refused to discuss the matter. Either the dealer has no knowledge of the value of that particular range of item, or else is unscrupulous enough to hope to thus make good his loss on some other article, and I have no wish to assist him to do so.

If, however, hallmarks indicate that a thimble is earlier than about 1840, one can think again. It may then be worth while starting to evaluate it in terms of £1·25 and upwards, depending on the quality, the rarity of design, the age, and finally (and perhaps most important of all) its appeal to one's own personal taste, and whether or not this is *the* thimble desired for a special box, or to complete a certain set of implements. The *price* paid then, as opposed to the *value*, will depend very largely on how much one wants that *particular* item. How much, in both senses, is the final criterion in the decision.

Since value, and price paid, seem such uncertain factors, the new collector may well inquire further, 'Then how am I to learn to discriminate between the valuable and the utterly worthless let alone between the good and the best?' The answer is that the very best way to start collecting any item, is to learn all one can about the subject, and at the same time see as many examples as possible in order ultimately to be able to make comparison between various specimens. I would suggest visiting museums, particularly those which specialise in workboxes, such as the Bethnal Green Museum in London which has a fine selection on public display. Many provincial museums and collections also have interesting examples, as also do some of the National Trust houses, and there are private collections in various places in England and abroad. The wider the field of comparison, the better the chance of assessing value fairly safely and (equally important) of knowing which particular type of accessory one wishes to collect. Gradually appreciation dawns that this or that particular type is met with fairly frequently, that it is nothing like so rare as at first appeared, and that therefore it is more likely to be available to a collector than other styles.

As a small personal instance of the sort of thing meant, the writer is very fond of mother-of-pearl. When, many years ago as a child, she first saw little mother-of-pearl reel-holders, their tops daintily ornamented with flower designs, she was immensely intrigued and thought that these must be rare and valuable. Had she been old enough to keep a diary, she might well have written about them in much the same glowing terms as Maria Russell wrote about her Indian box (page 151). But, years later, when she came to work in a well-known fine art auctioneer's and valuer's and, finally, to do research into thimbles and needlework accessories, she saw so many examples of these charming mother-of-pearl items that she came to realise that they are in fact comparatively common, and the sort of thing one might quite properly expect to collect by careful and judicious searching. What would be far more difficult to find, being much rarer, are those made of tortoiseshell, or even of finely damascened metals and other materials. Plain ivory ones are also comparatively common, but really beautifully carved ones in ivory are still not easy to find and would be a good buy.

The next stage is to decide what form the collection will take. Shall one start by collecting workboxes in general, of all styles and conditions, and then improve any which are slightly depleted by adding suitable fittings little by little? Or shall one start from the other end, so to speak, and collect individual accessories, working up until a fairly complete set has been achieved and only then seek a suitable box to house them, appropriate in style and period? Or, again, shall one decide to collect particular items, such as fine old shuttles, scissors, thimbles, or other special interests, having perhaps a historical background in mind, and hoping ultimately to go as far back as possible in the case of each item? To a great extent, in these days, any form of collecting is as much dependent upon the amount of space available for housing it as upon the amount of money to be expended on it. Ultimately it may well be the space problem which decides the form a collection is going to take.

Armed therefore with all the knowledge one has been able to acquire by seeing as many examples as possible of the different types of articles, and also, if possible, with a small pocket book giving the British assay office marks for silverware, one might now sally forth, albeit a little nervously, to try one's hand at purchasing in the chosen field. But exactly where is one to find that field. . . ? This is the main difficulty for a large number of would-be collectors.

If there are fairly large sums of money available, the most obvious step is to inquire of a reputable antique dealer. He will undoubtedly, within a few days or a week or two at most, be able to provide fairly expensive but fine, old boxes, dating from whatever period the collector may have stipulated. But in this case it is really the dealer who is having all the fun of the hide-and-seek part of the game we call 'collecting'. It might more properly be termed 'acquiring', and though the end results will be enjoyable, and often profitable in the long run, yet much of the fun will have been missed.

The second way available, is to inquire of all elderly relatives or friends whether they have any such boxes tucked away in cupboards or attics. It is surprising what a harvest this may well reap. Almost certainly, immediate reaction will be, that they can't remember anything like that at all. But wait a few days and often there will be a note or a phone call to say that they have been thinking about it and have remembered an old box Grandma used to have and which has now been traced up to the attics. By the time you get round to see it, as like as not they will have found a couple of others also, and their enthusiasm will not stop there. For the next few months boxes and cupboards, old trunks and drawers will be turned out and new finds will come your way— unless the infectious collecting bug has bitten them also. But at least your friends will be pleased that you started them off on a general spring-cleaning!

But the third and, to the writer's mind, the most useful and legitimate way, is to haunt local auctions and house-sales, and to see what they will yield. Even when, to one's dismay, a likely workbox or a bunch of accessories have been humped together with three firescreens, two brass gongs, a broken table lamp and a dog basket, and been avidly seized upon by some dealer, it is still often possible to approach him and buy the box or accessories privately before he leaves the sale. It leaves a feeling of real *bonhomie* on even the coldest winter's day—the dealer will have made a quick, on-the-spot turnover of items he might otherwise have had on his hands for weeks, so he will be happy, and the collector will be able to return home rejoicing. House-sales are a rich source of gain for collectors, and since many of the smaller items and accessories will come in a bundle of unsorted, often tangled, odds and ends, the sorting-through process will often be interesting as well as rewarding.

It is difficult to say exactly how plentiful various items will be. As in all fields, the more elaborate they are, the rarer they will be. Thus, an ivory shuttle for knotting and tatting may be found in almost every old box, but it will probably be a long haul before one finds a silver shuttle, or one in tortoiseshell, straw-work, mother-of-pearl and other materials. The really large, exquisitely worked ones of the days before the French Revolution will hardly ever be found in small sales, and even on the few occasions when they come up in the great auction houses of the world they will provoke fierce competition and fetch high prices. The average collector will usually have to be more modest in his hopes, and take his place in the queue for those which date from about 1780 onwards and are smaller, less elaborate and much less valuable. Again, it is difficult to assess prices accurately. A plain ivory shuttle bought in a box at a local house-sale might work out at 15p or 20p, whereas a dealer in a shop might ask anything from 50p to £2 ($1·20 to $4·80) for even the most ordinary type. Very much would depend on where his premises were, what his customers usually wanted, and how long he had had that particular item on his hands. On the other hand, a beautifully carved ivory tatting shuttle would be worth much more than that, and silver ones, though still comparatively common, would be well worth purchasing at anything from £3 ($7 or so) upwards, depending entirely on size, quality, decoration, etc.

When it comes to thimbles (see also page 79), again the date and material will make a wide difference to price. Derby, Rocking-ham, Sèvres and other china and porcelain thimbles which are a delight to any collector, are unfortunately very often cracked. Even then they will fetch £3 or £5 each at auction, depending, naturally, on the damage suffered, and the date and the make; but, if undamaged, most dealers will begin to talk in terms of £12, £20, and upwards to quite large sums. Care must always be taken to ensure that such thimbles are really old, and not modern ones, nor the ones turned out in some quantity at the beginning of this century. It is only a couple of years ago that, going through the stalls in one of London's open markets, I came across a modern china thimble similar to one my small son had proudly bought for me for Christmas in our local china shop for the princely sum of 10s (50p). This one had a different floral design on it, and I thought I would buy it, simply to keep the other company and to please him, so I inquired its price of the woman stall-holder. I would have been prepared to pay 62½p or 75p for it, making a small, but quick profit to her. But some very evident quick-thinking went on as she weighed me up and then fumbled through various sheets of paper, ostensibly looking up the price she had paid for it. Finally she said, 'Oh, yes, that one is Worcester, you can have it for £5, for a quick sale, though, really it is worth far more, I paid over £3 for it myself.' My reply was, 'In that case, I'm afraid you've made a bad buy, it's present-day Worcester, just check the mark inside, and you can buy them in most china shops for 10s.'

Although I love old and beautiful things, and have a deep respect for many dealers I have known, I still feel that one helps neither society nor the trade by paying unrealistic prices, more particularly when items are sold under any form of false pretence. It is simply tightening the noose about society's neck. Patience is a great part of the equipment a collector needs, and so is discernment! Knowledge of one's own particular subject is essential, and the ability to discriminate between realistic prices and those which are completely fanciful is of equal importance.

Turning to scissors, these will be more difficult to come by, largely because they take a good deal of strain, and therefore tended to become blunt or broken or to have the points snapped off if used for the wrong purposes, so that they were frequently thrown away. When really old and interesting pairs turn up in auctions they will probably already be collectors' pieces, and so the price they will command will be higher than for most items.

On the whole, there is no short cut to collecting needlework boxes and their contents. The collector staggering home with an old nineteenth-century workbox, picked up for £1·50, or $3 or $4, at a local auction, will be buying far more than the actual contents of the box. He will also be purchasing the sort of experience which comes only from the actual handling of different items, the *feel* of things—the feel and look of age. It is his best and surest way of increasing knowledge and perception. In just the same way an archaeologist, for instance, *feels* that a thing is, or is not, genuine. It may often be something he is not fully able to define in words at first, but there is that about an item which fits in with all his previous experience, or else it jars in some way with past recollection. To you and me, two objects may look exactly the same, but he will know, by the discernment gained over years of handling such items, that this one really did come from the Chaldean civilisation and that the other is a clever (probably *too*-clever) imitation made in the back streets of Birmingham or Paris. And in all fields the same thing is true. Thus, in a humbler sphere, the collector of workboxes and accessories will gradually come to have an affinity, almost an empathy, with the various items he comes across, and to know with some degree of accuracy their real age and monetary value, simply because of the many other similar items he has seen and handled, examined and compared. It is worth repeating that there is no better preparation than this in any area of collecting.

RENOVATING AND REPAIRING

Assuming that the new collector has now made a purchase, it may be as well to say something about the care of workboxes and their contents. Often the boxes come to one from years of neglect in an old attic or cupboard, or are bought at a sale with all their odds and ends jumbled up together, so that they are in sad need of repair and refurbishing. In this event, it is easy either to discard them entirely as beyond redemption, or else to rip away the old worn silks and velvets with which they were originally lined, and, if sufficiently industrious, to reline them completely. There are different schools of thought about this latter procedure. Personally, it always seems to the writer a shame to throw away the original linings unless they are so rotted and worn that they are totally useless. Very often a little careful brushing, where velvet and fairly strong materials are concerned, is sufficient to make a marked improvement. Silks can be treated with the care and gentleness one would show to the sick and frail, and be sponged down with soap and water, or a little borax in water (detergents are liable to damage the materials and fade the colours where old fabrics are concerned). It is surprising what a difference such treatment can make to the feel as well as the look of fabrics.

Old, neglected wood can be wonderfully restored by a little thought and trouble. Where it is greasy from old polish it can be sponged down, very gently and carefully, ensuring that the grease be taken off but not the underlying veneer or polish. Dried with a soft, warm cloth, it is then ready for polishing. Where years of neglect have taken their toll it will be as well to make this a daily practice for a while, though only putting on polish at the beginning and perhaps once a month or so afterwards. More things have been ruined through too much polish and grease accruing on them than many people realise. The gentle friction of a soft cloth is quite sufficient polish for most days and it is the constant care, rather than the occasional liberal splash of spray or wax, which will bring back the warm, high gleam of the wood.

If the compartments are lined with paper, this should be carefully stuck back into place where damaged, unless it is really beyond hope, when the whole section may need re-lining. In this case, it is a good thing to examine each piece, see how it was originally put on and then cut the new lining in the same style and fix it accordingly.

Few people realise that ivory needs sunlight to keep it in good condition. Kept in the dark, it soon turns yellow and loses its lustre. A safe cleanser may be made by using a little whitening moistened with lemon juice and made into a fine paste. This can be rubbed on with a chamois leather and left to dry, when it will brush off easily and the ivory can be polished with a soft cloth or leather. Here again, some people use borax, which is a safe cleanser for many articles, but the main thing is that sunlight should be allowed to get to the ivory from time to time and it should not be constantly in darkness or even semi-darkness.

Mother-of-pearl needs little to restore it, apart from a regular light rub now and again.

Stains on silver may sometimes be removed by using whitening moistened with methylated spirit, or else ammonia, and then cleaning in the ordinary way. The various proprietary brands of tarnish removers and silver polishers available today may be used fairly safely, but some old stains are difficult to remove and it may be as well not to deal too drastically with them, and to make sure first of all that the article really *is* silver.

Japanned and papiermâché boxes may be sponged down with a little lukewarm water and then dried thoroughly. Never allow very hot, or boiling, water to touch any of the japanned-ware articles, since it will crack the varnish and make it peel. A little polish and then a regular brushing or rubbing with a soft cloth will improve old japanned boxes considerably.

Where leather has been used for any of the interior fittings of a box it may well be old and dry. In this case it can be softened with a little fine oil and rubbed down with a sponge dipped in turps, and finally given a thin coat of clear polish. Be careful not to put this on in dabs, or it will leave dark spots where first deposited, and always use it sparingly at any one time. A good reviver for leather is to take about a third of a pint of vinegar and two-thirds of a pint of boiled linseed oil. Shake these together in a bottle until of the consistency of cream, then rub carefully into the leather and polish with a soft duster.

Many people use a little warm water, with sour milk or lemon juice added to it, to bring back the gloss to lacquered goods. Rub them down with a piece of soft flannel or silk, dry in a warm place and then polish with a chamois leather.

A little judicious use of some of the excellent fixatives now on sale will repair and renew many of the old fitments which may have become cracked, loose, or otherwise damaged.

Many collectors dislike the idea of renewing and mending old materials and fitments, but it is probable that a distinguishing line may be drawn between two types of collecting. Clearly a beautiful, really old case can just be treated carefully and yet be as near as possible to its original state. But there are many boxes which must either have a little rehabilitation or else be completely discarded, and since so many old things have already been lost or destroyed, it seems to the writer that, whenever possible, every effort should be made to preserve and renew whatever remains. This applies particularly to the very many old, late Victorian boxes most collectors may come across. Often they are in a worse state than their earlier companions, and have more utensils missing or broken. Nevertheless, they have a value in their own right, and can add interest and enjoyment to the whole of a collection. Indeed, part of a collector's joy, may well lie in the painstaking and loving care given to old, fragile items, and the joy of seeing them blossom out anew, as though in gratitude for the time and energy expended on them. In this respect, the collector who is able to afford to buy only the finest and most perfect specimens, is, in one sense, less fortunate than his humbler brother who, like the Good Samaritan, knows the joy of a rescue job well done.

To all those who collect and love needlework boxes, their tools and myriad contents, I would wish good hunting, success in their quest, and great joy eventually in their possessions.

GLOSSARY

Carnet de bal   A dance programme. A small pocket-book usually with covers of mother-of-pearl, ivory, etc, in which a lady wrote the names of her dance partners for each dance of the evening, and which later evolved into the ordinary small card dance-programmes used in this century.

Chasing   This is a process similar to engraving, but the ornamental designs produced upon the surface of the work are all raised or embossed. A special set of tools is used for this work, mainly carried out by silversmiths.

Ear-spoon   A small spoon, similar to that used for taking snuff but, where ears were concerned, kept for medicinal usage in pouring in oil or removing wax.

Engraving   Producing a fine tracery upon metal by cutting in with small gouges or needles.

Harewood   Sycamore wood stained with oxide of iron until a greenish grey in colour; used frequently as a veneer during second half of eighteenth century.

Intaglio   The exact opposite of a design in relief. The design is engraved, cut, or incised into very hard material and is below the surface level of the material into which it is cut.

Latten   A mixed metal of yellowish colour resembling brass, much used in England until about the sixteenth century. Essentially it is composed of an impure mixture of brass, in which unrefined zinc was used to blend with the copper, whereas in brass the zinc was purified.

Marquetry   A type of veneer in which shaped pieces of different coloured woods are combined to form a design and laid on a surface of glue. Marquetry was unknown in England until the

171

Restoration in 1660, but became extremely popular during the reigns of William and Mary and Queen Anne.

Paste A hard, vitreous composition used in making imitation gems. Refers more particularly to the imitation diamonds popular in the eighteenth and nineteenth centuries and is sometimes known also as strasse or strass, after Joseph Strasser, who, in the middle of the eighteenth century, discovered a way of making pieces of faceted lead glass which, when set in foil in a silver or pewter mounting, formed a very satisfactory imitation of a diamond. True early paste has quite a considerable value in its own right and can normally be recognised by the fact that the stones are usually in a sunken mounting and held in place by small chips or grains of metal.

Pinchbeck An alloy composed of 3 parts zinc and 4 parts copper. It was much used for fine watch cases, chatelaines, etui, etc, and was invented by Christopher Pinchbeck, 1670–1732. It is initially the colour of old brass, but when polished gives a soft, warm, golden effect.

Pounce A fine powder made from pulverised *gum sandarac*, a resin from a NW African tree. Used to stop ink spreading on unsized paper; also when tracing designs for embroidery, when it may be made from powdered charcoal.

Pounce-box or pounce-pot A sand castor, containing pounce, and usually found in writing boxes or with writing materials.

Pouncet-box A small box with perforated lid, used for perfumes, etc, and the forerunner of the vinaigrette.

Pouncing The small punched indentations on a thimble; the word comes from 'punch' or 'punching'.

Repoussé A design on a metal object hammered into relief from the reverse side of the metal. Bronze, brass, gold and silver are all especially suitable for repoussé designs.

Rosewood A hard wood, *dalbergia nigra*, dark red streaked with black, used for inlay and cabinetwork in the eighteenth century, usually combined with satinwood. After 1800 rosewood became popular in its own right and many Regency pieces were made entirely of rosewood. Used in America from c 1845–60.

Satinwood From an E Indian tree, *chlorxylon swietenia*. Hard, and
has yellow-gold colouring and wavy veining. There is also a
Florida variety which gives a slightly orange colour, and the
Red Satinwood of the W Indies is red, veined with yellow.
Much used from c 1770 in conjunction with veneers of other
colouring and with stained woods such as mahogany, rosewood, ebony, harewood, stained holly.

Shagreen Originally untanned leather from the hide of a horse or
wild ass obtained from Persia and Turkey. The artificially
grained surface on early seventeenth-century shagreen was
made by pressing small seeds into skins whilst still soft and
flexible. After various processes they were dyed green or black
and dried, when they became very firm. Used widely in
England in Jacobean times but less so during the nineteenth
century. Later shagreen was made from highly polished skins
of seals, sharks and other fish.

Snuff-spoon Usually made in silver, for taking snuff. A small
quantity was taken from the box with the spoon and placed on
the back of the left hand, or between the thumb and forefinger and then sniffed up the nostrils.

Straw-work For this type of work, straw is split into convenient
lengths then bleached, dyed and, with the aid of an adhesive,
laid on the surface of the article to be decorated. The vari-
coloured straws are laid in different directions so that the
light catches squares and oblongs at different angles, the
honey-coloured shades offset by the deeper-dyed straws making a charming effect.

Stumpwork A form of embroidery popular during fifteenth and
seventeenth centuries, where most of the design is done in
relief. The raised, often flexible, parts of the design are produced by building up a foundation of cotton or wool and then
covering it with material. The hand or arm, for instance, of a
person worked in stumpwork will quite literally 'stand out'
from the body of the work and will have a sleeve and suitable
laces or trimmings worked on it just as if it were part of a
doll.

Tent stitch Sometimes referred to as petit point. The finest of the
English canvas stitches and the direction of the work is from

the top right hand to the bottom left. When crossed by another stitch it forms cross stitch or gros point.

Vernis martin A type of French lacquer work which differs from the method used in oriental lacquer and derives from the French word for varnish.

Verre églomise Glass ornamented by having a drawing and painting made, the underside of which is then backed with metal foil, or gold or silver leaf. Originated by Jean Baptiste Blomi, c 1786.

BIBLIOGRAPHY

Albert, L. S. and Kent, K. *The Complete Button Book* (New York 1949)

D'Allemagne, H. R. *Les Accessoires du Coutume et du Mobilier* (Paris 1928)

Fastnedge, R. *Sheraton Furniture* (1962)

Forbes, R. J. *Studies in Ancient Technology* (New York 1964)

Groves, S. *The History of Needlework Tools and Accessories* (1969)

Kybalova, L. etc. *Pictorial Encyclopaedia of Fashion* (1969)

Liversidge, J. *Britain in the Roman Empire* (1968)

Longman, E. D. and Loch, S. *Pins and Pincushions* (1911)

Oxford Dictionary of Historic Principles

Peacock, Primrose. *Buttons for the Collector* (Newton Abbot 1971)

Ward, J. *The Roman Era in Britain* (1911)

Whiting, G. *Tools and Toys of Stitchery* (New York 1925)

Yarwood, D. *The English Home* (1956)

ACKNOWLEDGEMENTS

Usually the public regards the author of a book as the person who has written it and, in the strictly mechanical sense, this is true. But, in the wider sense, a book is a combined work, produced very largely by the generous assistance of many people who have given of their time, knowledge and experience, or loaned their personal possessions, in order to enrich the writer's own slender resources. It is this readiness to share knowledge, to help with technical skills, and to give encouragement of every sort, which makes the work of writing a book truly enjoyable, in spite of the many difficulties and set-backs involved. Because of this, I should like to express my most grateful thanks to all the following.

To the Welsh Folk Museum at St Fagans (National Museum of Wales) and to the State Historical Museum, Moscow, for permission to reproduce certain plates. To Mr Stephen Essberger, who has taken all the remaining plates, and to whom I owe an especial debt of gratitude for travelling to many different parts of the country in order to photograph different items, and for arranging and displaying the small individual accessories with such great care, patience and skill. Many of the photographs he took could not be included here because of space problems, but they have been most helpful in enabling me to make sketches for the illustrations when my visual memory might well have failed me.

I am also most grateful to all those individuals who have so kindly allowed me to examine the many different articles in their possession, have helped me with details and information and, in many cases, have also allowed photographs to be taken. In this connection I would particularly mention Miss M. Biddulph; Mr and Mrs H. Cotton, whose private collection of Victoriana furnished most interesting and enlightening details in many directions; Miss Primrose Peacock; Mrs Elizabeth Sowdon and the Misses Sowdon; Miss B. H. Ward of Peterstow; Miss Gwenllian Williams of Chislehurst, Kent; and Mrs Dorothy Wiseman of Hay-on-Wye. To the curators and assistants of the various National Trust properties which house examples of needlework boxes and tables and various contents, I also wish to tender my sincere thanks for kindness and willing co-operation.

Especial thanks are due also to the many officers of museums who have given me help both by correspondence, and also by personal assistance on the spot in sorting through and producing from their deposits the many items (not always mentioned, sadly enough, since space precluded) which have enabled me to compare, classify and check not only the different styles of workboxes and tables, but also the wide assortment of items included in them. Such thanks are especially due to Dr Ilid Anthony of the National Folk Museum of Wales, St Fagans; Dr H. Savory and his assistants at the National Museum of Wales, Cardiff; Miss Pamela Clabburn, of Stranger's Hall Museum, Norwich; Mr D. King, Deputy Keeper of the Department of Textiles at the Victoria & Albert Museum, London; Mrs L. Webster, Assistant Keeper of the Department of Medieval & Later Antiquities of the British Museum; Miss Jennifer H. S. Minay of the Gloucester Folk Museum; Miss M. Archibald, Curator of Blakesley Hall, City of Birmingham Museums; Mrs Gonan of the American Museum, Bath; Mr J. R. Holmes, Assistant Keeper of the London Museum; Mr G. C. Boon, FSA, for permission to give details of his Roman knitting needle 'find'; the Curator of the State Historical Museum, Moscow; Dr T. Hausmann of the Kunstgewerbemuseum, Berlin; and the Curator of the German National Museum, Nuremberg.

No one can do research work without realising how greatly he depends on the staff of our libraries and their untiring efforts. In this connection, I would acknowledge my indebtedness to the staff of all those libraries whom I have haunted, harried and harassed over the years with requests for elusive books and long forgotten magazine articles, especially the staff of Anerley Public

Acknowledgements

Library; Beckenham Public Library; the British Museum Library; Bromley Public Library; Gloucester City Library; the Guildhall Library, London; Hereford County Library and the City of Westminster Library. Simply because, in a book of this length it is impossible to fit in all the details and knowledge gathered from their efforts, much may appear to have been wasted and ignored. This is not so—knowledge is passed on in a hundred other ways beside the printed page. Because of this I would like all those mentioned above to know that what they have given will always be handed on to others whenever possible, and, like a ripple on a pond, their kindness and effort will spread wider than they suspect.

In closing, I should also like to thank my publishers, David & Charles, for their patient help with my queries and various problems, together with all my many friends who have given encouragement and reassurance when my ardour seemed to flag.

INDEX

References to illustrations are printed in italics. Many articles can also be seen in the plates showing complete workbox interiors

Index